I0409461

THE BOOK OF KASPA

Realizing the Nakamoto Dream

N. R. CROWNINGSHIELD

1 N. R. Crowningshield

To my guiding star, Lisa, and our endless source of joy, Finley.

Let this book testify to my love and dedication as I imbue it on

every page.

A heartfelt thank you to the Kaspa Community,

whose unwavering support turned this dream into reality.

Your faith in me echoes in each word.

3   N. R. Crowningshield

Contents

7   N. R. Crowningshield

The Book of Kaspa 8

9   N. R. Crowningshield

Foreword

The unpredictable, ever-evolving universe of cryptocurrency is teeming with opportunities ripe for exploration. Like budding celestial bodies on the brink of either burning out or becoming blazing suns, each spark in this cosmic conundrum holds explosive, transformative, and sometimes fleeting potential. On this celestial journey, I chanced upon a newborn star, Kaspa. This chance encounter set my course toward an unexpected, exhilarating adventure.

In the historical backdrop of this interstellar adventure, a monumental shift occurred in the Ethereum galaxy. The consensus mechanism, the beating heart of Ethereum, was morphing from the industrious, labor-intensive proof-of-work to the sleek, energy-conscious proof-of-stake. In this storm of change, I gravitated towards the vibrant, chaotic charm of Kaspa's Discord community. I entered this brave new world under the colorful moniker of Bubblegum Lightning. The scene I encountered was nothing short of a socio-technical rendition of Lord of the Flies, exuding all the charm of a live prison takeover.

Intrigued but overwhelmed, I tucked Kaspa into the back pocket of my attention. I had a more pressing matter at hand, another newcomer who had entered my gravity well: my son, who made his grand entrance into the world on November 9th, 2022. As anyone who has navigated the vague territory of new parenthood can tell you, falling in love with your tiny cohabitant is a full-time job.

But as December unfolded, my pint-sized doppelganger seemed to reassign my role in our tiny universe. I was no longer just 'Dad'; I had evolved into a comfy, body-heated mattress and, at other times, an on-demand waste disposal system. Consequently, my couch and I entered a serious relationship, with this little guy forming a warm, wriggling cocoon on my chest. My wakeful hours expanded, and with them, my intrigue for Kaspa started to gnaw at me again. Thankfully, I had a gateway to the world, right in the form of a hand-held techno-marvel – the smartphone. Gotta love technology.

My initial fascination with Kaspa had been piqued by the visualizer of the unique blockDAG structure, a harmonious blend of technical innovation and creative thought. I found myself transfixed as I watched the blockchain fracture and then recompose into a chain. It was fascinating. Yet, as I devoted more time to uncover its mysteries, it revealed itself as something more extraordinary than just this wild blockchain-DAG hybrid thing. It was a cryptographic masterpiece, a meticulously woven tapestry of code that might give Vincent van Gough second thoughts about the whole ear thing.

With a newfound determination to peel back the layers, I plunged into the belly of the beast, hoping to quench my thirst for knowledge. But my quest for learning hit a snag. The Kaspa community, much like my son, was still in its infancy, toddling along the road of evolution. Resources for education were few and far between. To my shock and slight horror, Kaspa didn't even have a Medium page – a basic lifeline in the choppy seas of the crypto. I mean, even the meme-spawned Dogecoin had one!

But then, just as I was about to drift into the void of disillusionment, I encountered Super Moderator Tim (well, he's just a mod now, but that's a story for another day). He was a beacon of enlightenment in the treacherous, foggy waters of the internet. It turned out that the lack of a Medium page was startlingly simple – nobody had thought to create one yet. Probably because they were too busy making NFTs or something.

Before me lay a blank canvas, waiting for the first brushstroke of my contribution. I eagerly stepped up to the challenge like a hyperactive kid on the first day of school, armed with a brand-new set of glitter pens. Contributing to something grander than myself was exciting. I could mold it into something the Kaspa ethos would expect and appreciate. Open-source, inclusive, and organic.

Starting the Kaspa Currency Medium page was like mounting an expedition into an unknown land. I dusted off my writing skills, cobweb-laden from years of disuse, and steered them toward non-fiction. The transition from spinning tales in the whimsical realms of fiction to articulating non-fiction's hard, unyielding facts felt like swapping a soft-down pillow for a concrete slab. My early posts resembled an alien language more than coherent, engaging content.

Yet, to my amazement, the Kaspa community rallied behind me. They devoured my posts, quoted my words, and created videos based on the information I was publishing. The once vacant Medium page had blossomed into a bustling hub of intellectual exchange, a beacon for new users, budding developers, and crypto enthusiasts alike.

Amid this whirlwind journey, I received a transmission from a fellow Kaspanaut named Potat, who enlisted my assistance for a post on r/cryptocurrency. Although I didn't have an active comlink with them, I agreed to co-pilot the writing expedition. We battled through language barriers and the unruly beast of content preferences. Despite these adversities, we persevered, ultimately forging an article that satisfied the stringent standards of r/cryptocurrency.

Then the day arrived when Potat posted our collective effort, and it took off like the Saturn V rocket. The upvotes poured in like a meteor shower in a clear night sky, with Potat excitedly broadcasting each milestone on our Telegram channel—100, 200, 500, 1000—as if we were astronomers cataloging new stars in the cosmos. It was an almost surreal, dizzying experience; Potat and I, just a pair of ordinary Joes, were unexpectedly propelled into the spotlight. Yet, we didn't stand alone. With the buoyant support of our community (which came from nowhere and in every direction), we rose to the occasion, answering subreddit users' inquiries, engaging in rich discussions, and drawing an ever-increasing sphere of attention.

Then, our joyride ended as abruptly as a slap to the face. The post was deleted, and an unforgiving wave of bans took us all down, Potat included. Apparently, our crime was discussing Kaspa; imagine that, a subreddit about crypto. which the sub-mods had dismissively labeled as a "shitcoin." Their reaction served to only solidify my belief in Kaspa's potential. If the threat of Kaspa overtaking their dying assets rattled them this much, Kaspa was definitely onto something revolutionary.

The aftermath of the deletion catapulted Potat and me into unexpected fame. By request, my repertoire of responsibilities expanded to include hosting Twitter Spaces, participating in AMAs, moderating Discord and Telegram, troubleshooting, and even organizing and smoothing operations. All voluntary, of course, I don't have to, but the community likes it, and I love that they do. All at the community's request. I even gained the self-proclaimed title of PR manager and copywriter. The traditional world likes their labels, though they mean nothing in Kaspaland.

My humble Medium page evolved into publishing for the Kaspa CoinMarketCap page, and I soon found a home on Kaspa.org/news. I was becoming a cog in the decentralized machinery.

And then, amid my crazy Kaspa ventures, someone asked me to write a book...

17 N. R. Crowningshield

Chapter 1

Barter, Beads, and Banks

The concept of money has a weird way of making you feel like you're caught in an arbitrary whirlwind. Earning money by making a living and then spending earned money to live. Rinse and repeat until the end of days. It's a story almost as old as humankind itself. It can all feel depressing, yet, when you think about it, bewildering, from shells and beads to metal coins and paper money to the digital realm of cryptocurrencies. So why do we need money? Does it have any real point? What the hell does equity mean? Let's dive into this peculiar and perplexing system of mysteries and find out. And let's give particular attention to silver, as it has played a crucial role in our narrative. After all, silver has not only been a driving force in the development of currency systems throughout history, but it's also the very foundation upon which the Kaspa currency stands.

Starting off with the controversial yet textbook beginning: bartering. In all its charming simplicity, the barter system was a bit of a mess, if I'm being honest. Trading goods and services directly, without any standardized currency, led to a heap of problems that made groceries and shopping one big headache. The most significant issue plaguing the barter system was what those fancy economists call the "double coincidence of wants."

Picture this: you're a farmer with a crop of apples and looking to trade them for some wheat. Of course, the real kicker here is finding someone who not only has wheat to spare but who also happens to be in the market for apples. Both parties need to have a want for the other's goods; thus, a double coincidence of wants. If no one wants your apples or has any wheat, your apple pie plans are ruined.

The inefficiencies of the barter system weren't just limited to the double coincidence of wants, either. Establishing a fair exchange rate for various goods and services was also subjective and unrealistic. For instance, how many sacks of wheat would equal the value of a bushel of apples?

Depending on supply and demand, desperation or lack thereof would make for a highly volatile food market.

Likewise, trying to store value for future use was an exercise in futility. Imagine stashing a barn full of apples, hoping they'll retain their value over the following years. Depending on pests, environmental conditions, and bad actors, your hard-earned apples could depreciate randomly and in the blink of an eye. Just like the overripe bananas, you could have sworn they were green just yesterday.

Suddenly and thankfully, the Big Bang of finance happened, and commodity money burst onto the scene, forever changing how humans traded. Shells, beads, salt, and a whole assortment of items with intrinsic value suddenly became the go-to currencies of the day. These commodities were universally recognized and accepted, which meant that trading became a whole lot easier.

Let there be commerce!

With the arrival of commodity money, the double coincidence of wants problem faded fast. People no longer had to scramble around, trying to find one person who both wanted their goods and had something they needed in return. Now your apple crop could be assigned a value in salt. You could then exchange that salt for wheat or even store it until you are ready to buy wheat without timing the apple's spoilage. Commodity money greases the wheels of commerce, allowing people to exchange goods and services with relative ease.

It's important to note that not all commodity money was created equal. Some items were undoubtedly more practical than others for use as currency. Shells and beads, for example, were lightweight and portable but lacked durability. On the other hand, salt was valuable but difficult to store and transport. Getting caught in the rain with a year's harvest worth of wages in salt would not be a good time. But fear not, intrepid explorers of trade, for our story doesn't end there.

Now, metal coins were kind of a big deal. They were durable, easy to transport, and could be divided into smaller denominations to suit various transactions. Gold and silver coins in particular were the stars of the show. Gold was highly valued, no doubt, and great for a few large transactions, such as buying real estate or a ship. However, it was silver that really shined when it came to everyday transactions. Its lower value and abundance compared to gold made it accessible to the common folk, sparking economic growth and laying the foundations for international trade networks.

One of the earliest examples of silver coins can be traced back to the ancient kingdom of Lydia, nestled in what is now modern-day Turkey. Around 600 BCE, those clever Lydians started producing standardized mints made from electrum, a naturally occurring alloy of gold and silver. These coins proudly displayed the image of a lion—a symbol of strength, authority, and the beginning of old movies. And, as it often happens with great ideas, it wasn't long before other civilizations, like the Greeks, Romans, and Persians, jumped on the bandwagon and began using silver coinage adorned with their own iconic (probably inferior) animals as their primary currency.

Now, I don't want to give the impression that other metals weren't used for coinage. Oh no, they certainly had their time in the sun. But silver's corrosion resistance, malleability, and adaptability made it second to none. The other metals all failed to make the same impact or generate the sheer volume of transactions that silver did. Silver was the MVP of the ancient currency world.

The widespread adoption of silver coins was an absolute game-changer. It provided a more stable and predictable store of value, encouraging savings, investment, and long-term planning. But that's not all! Silver coins also facilitated the development of global trade networks by providing a universally recognized medium of exchange that could be used to conduct transactions across different societies and cultures.

Getting bored of the silver shill? Why all the focus on silver? Well, silver plays a crucial role in our story, and it's not just because of its historical significance. There's a connection between silver and Kaspa; that intriguing new cryptocurrency I mentioned earlier. But don't worry, I'll dive deeper into that later. For now, silver's unique properties, widespread use, and support for many transactions have a few lessons to teach us about the evolution of currency and how Kaspa aims to revolutionize the world of digital money. So, stick around as we continue this thrilling ride through the history of currency!

Modern Money
As with everything in life, things never stay the same for long. Society continued to evolve and so too did its currency systems. The transition from metal coins to paper money marked a significant

shift in how people conducted trade and stored wealth.

The story of paper money can be traced back to ancient China during the Sui Dynasty (581–618 AD). Initially, paper money was used as a form of promissory notes, representing a guarantee to pay the bearer a specific amount of metal coins upon demand. Over time, paper money gained popularity and people began using it as a medium of exchange instead of metal coins. This shift brought about several advantages. For one, paper money was lighter and easier to transport, making it more convenient for large transactions. Moreover, printing different denominations allowed for more precise control over the money supply, which helped stabilize economies and prevent inflation. Also, a more straightforward and larger canvas for bigger pictures of animals, probably.

As paper money started making waves in the 17th century, banks and governments found themselves front and center in the more influential world of money. So, they put on their fancy wigs and clothes and started issuing and regulating these newfangled banknotes while keeping a keen eye on the value and stability of their currencies through some nifty monetary policies and money supply control.

Over in Europe, the Bank of Sweden got the ball rolling by issuing paper money in 1661, with the Bank of England following suit in 1694. These early banknotes were backed by shiny precious metals like gold and silver, creating a stable and predictable store of value perfect for nurturing economic growth and stability.

The adoption of the gold and silver standards varies across countries and regions; however, at some point, they became devotees of the Cult of Gold. The United Kingdom, always eager to be ahead of the curve, adopted the gold standard in 1821, while the United States took its sweet time and didn't jump on the bandwagon until 1879. The 19th century saw the gold standard become all the rage, with countries around the globe scrambling to adopt the system and maintain confidence in their respective currencies.

The telegraph had already been zapping messages across continents, and now the telephone was making long-distance communication as easy as pie. Long-distance transportation and commerce were becoming more accessible and more efficient, International trade was booming, and the world needed a more flexible and responsive monetary system.

Meanwhile, the world of banking was evolving at breakneck speed. Banks were getting creative with their services, offering everything from loans and mortgages to investment products and payment processing. As globalization picked up steam, banks started to cozy up to each other, working together to facilitate international trade and finance.

Speaking of banks, let's not forget the birth of modern banking and the creation of the Federal Reserve System in the United States in 1913. This game-changing innovation helped stabilize the US economy and prevent bank panics, providing a framework for monetary policy that's still in play today. The Fed's role in managing the money supply and keeping inflation in check has been crucial for maintaining global and national economic stability.

Nevertheless, the gold standard started to crack under the pressure of global events like World War I and the Great Depression. As a result, governments began to abandon it in favor of more flexible monetary policies. This led to a new chapter in the currency story, as the Bretton Woods system took center stage, and the US dollar became the world's reserve currency.

Delegates from forty-four nations gathered in the sleepy New Hampshire town of Bretton Woods in 1944, hashing out a new framework for international monetary cooperation. They wanted to create a more stable and predictable system to support global economic growth and prevent further chaos similar to what they'd just lived through.

The Bretton Woods system had a couple of crucial components. First, it pegged other currencies to the US dollar, which was, in turn, pegged to gold. This meant that countries could exchange their dollars for gold at a fixed rate, effectively making the US dollar the world's reserve currency. Second, the system created two new institutions: the International Monetary Fund (IMF) and the World Bank. These organizations provided financial support and guidance to countries in need, helping stabilize the global economy and promote development.

However, the Bretton Woods system wasn't perfect, a common theme in finance. In the 1960s, inflation started gnawing away at the value of the US dollar, and doubts began to creep in about the system's sustainability. In 1971, President Nixon dropped the mic: the US would no longer convert dollars into gold, effectively severing the link between the dollar and gold. This marked the end of the Bretton Woods system and the era of the gold standard.

Despite its eventual collapse, the Bretton Woods system had a lasting impact on the global economy. It ushered in a new era of international cooperation and helped lay the groundwork for the modern financial and banking systems that we know and love/hate today. As a result, banks became more sophisticated, offering various financial services, from advanced loans and mortgages to investment products and payment processing. With the rise of globalization, banking also became even more interconnected, with banks working together on a global scale to facilitate international trade and finance.

Perhaps the most significant development in banking was the move toward electronic and digital money. As computers and the internet became increasingly prevalent, banks started to digitize their services. This meant that money could be transferred electronically, making transactions faster and more convenient. People no longer had to carry around wads of cash or physically visit a bank to deposit a check. Debit and credit features now fit in the convenience of a thin plastic card.

Companies like CyberCash, PayPal, Square, and other online payment systems emerged, allowing individuals and businesses to send and receive money with just a few clicks of a button. Online banking became the norm, and the use of physical cash started to decline. All of this set the stage for the next big revolution in currency—the magic internet money known as cryptocurrency.

Cryptocurrencies, like Bitcoin and Ethereum, use decentralized networks of computers to maintain a transparent and secure ledger of transactions. As a result, they're not controlled by any single entity, and their value is determined by supply and demand. As intriguing as these digital currencies are, they've faced their fair share of challenges, such as volatile prices, network difficulties, and scalability issues.

The Crypto Future

So here we are, all caught up and in the 21st century, with a plethora of ways to pay for goods and services. We've got cash, credit and debit cards, digital wallets, and now cryptocurrencies. It's a far cry from the days of bartering and paying with seashells. Still, the underlying principles remain the same—money is a tool for facilitating trade. At the end of the day, its value is ultimately determined by the trust we place in it.

As we move further into the digital age, it's worth considering what the future of currency might look like. Will cryptocurrencies like Kaspa become the dominant form of money, or will they exist alongside traditional fiat currencies? Could we see the return of asset-backed currencies, like gold and silver standards or a cutting-edge seashell standard? Will governments continue to wield control over money supplies through fiat currency systems?

These are the questions that will undoubtedly shape the course of human history in the coming decades. But one thing is sure–currency's evolution is far from over. From shells and beads to silver coins, paper money, cryptocurrencies, and now Kaspa, the story of money is a fascinating reflection of the ever-changing human experience.

Kaspa's story, however, has just begun.

Chapter 2

The Bitcoin and Ethereum Dichotomy Dilemma

In the year of our Satoshi 2009, Lady Gaga's "Poker Face" plays on the radio for the seventh time today, you're falling behind on your FarmVille agribusiness, and the world is in an economic mess. The global economy teetered on the edge of collapse, and trust in financial institutions had plunged to an all-time low. So, naturally, people craved a solution to the turmoil, and that's when a shadowy figure—or perhaps a group of figures—emerged from the digital ether.

This enigmatic individual (or collective or Yonatan?) called themselves Satoshi Nakamoto, and they bore a gift for the world: a whitepaper that would forever change the financial landscape. The document outlined the genesis of a new kind of currency, one that didn't rely on intermediaries like banks or payment processors. It was called Bitcoin.

This wasn't like your PayPals and Venmos, where you sent and received fiat currency across cyberspace. Bitcoin was an actual digital currency—a cryptocurrency, if you will—that harnessed a fancy new technology called the blockchain. The blockchain was an immutable public ledger that allowed transactions to be recorded transparently, securely, and without a central authority. It was as if someone had taken the best parts of a bank, a safe, and a postal service, thrown them into a blender, and hit "puree." And then, in a genuine badass decentralized manner, this someone boldly decided to abandon the digital smoothie entirely. Either intentionally or unintentionally.

As Bitcoin emerged from the primordial digital milkshake, people began to take notice. They started to use it as a means of exchange, and its value began to rise. It was the first of its kind, a true pioneer in the World of the Wide Web.

The blockchain technology that powered Bitcoin was a stroke of genius. A ledger that everyone could see but no one could change without the approval of the majority. It was a system that favored trust, cooperation, and decentralization. Transactions were recorded in "blocks," which were then linked together in a "chain" that grew longer and more robust as time passed.

But like any good story, this one had its share of twists and turns. As people began to adopt Bitcoin, they also started to poke at its limitations. The system was slooow and cumbersome, bogged down by its own security measures. It was like trying to run a marathon during the height of COVID while wearing three masks, a hazmat suit, and a face shield while huffing hand sanitizer. Not very sustainable.

Yet the idea of a decentralized digital currency had taken root. Bitcoin was no longer an obscure experiment but a force to be reckoned with. It had broken the mold, and in doing so, it opened the door to a new world of possibilities. People began to dream of a financial system free from the shackles of banks and governments, a system as vast and untamed as the "free market."

In the wake of Bitcoin's revolutionary birth, the digital landscape evolved from the blockchain foundation. New possibilities and opportunities beckoned, and fresh-faced explorers emerged, eager to stake their claims in the uncharted territories of decentralized digital finance. Among them was a young visionary named Vitalik Buterin.

Now, Vitalik wasn't content with merely participating in the crypto gold rush. He had loftier ambitions. Inspired by the groundbreaking achievements of Bitcoin, he set out to develop a new kind of decentralized platform that would expand upon the original vision of Bitcoin and push the boundaries of what was possible with blockchain technology.

Vitalik's brainchild was Ethereum, a decentralized platform that allowed developers to create their own applications powered by a new cryptocurrency called ETH. Ethereum wasn't just a cryptocurrency; it was a digital playground, an open-source sandbox that beckoned programmers from all corners of the globe to come and live their sweet cyber dreams.

In 2015, Ethereum finally launched, and it was like someone had taken COVID and made it a computer virus. Except the digital world was hyped instead of quarantined, and they had plenty of toilet paper for a new era of innovation to begin. Ethereum's unique selling point was the introduction of "smart contracts"—self-executing contracts that ran on the blockchain, making transactions transparent, trustless, and secure.

This innovation opened the door to a multitude of possibilities. Decentralized finance—or DeFi, as the cool kids called it—was now possible. DeFi applications allow users to participate in financial activities, like lending, borrowing, and trading, without the need for traditional intermediaries like banks. It was as if someone had handed the economic power back to the people, and they took off running with it.

The Ethereum platform also gave rise to non-fungible tokens, or NFTs, like digital collectibles on steroids. These unique digital assets could represent anything from digital art to virtual real estate and were bought, sold, and traded on various marketplaces. Each NFT was like a one-of-a-kind snowflake, a unique and indivisible piece of digital property authenticated and secured by the Ethereum blockchain.

From primitive smoothie to virtual gold rush, Bitcoin and Ethereum's value skyrocketed, as did the number of eager prospectors seeking to stake their claim in the digital Wild West. But as with any gold rush, the rapid influx of participants unearthed some fool's gold and unsustainable ground. Bitcoin, the original trailblazer of the cryptocurrency world, was beginning to show signs of strain under the weight of its own success.

Bitcoin's scalability issues are rooted in its Proof-of-Work consensus mechanism. PoW required miners to solve complex mathematical puzzles to validate transactions and add new blocks to the blockchain. While this method provided robust security, it was also incredibly energy-intensive and placed a hard cap on the number of transactions that could be processed per second. Its block size limit permitted only one MB blocks every ten minutes. Chump change/data in this day and age.

As the digital highways of Bitcoin grew ever more congested, proposed solutions to the scalability problem began to increase. One such solution was the Lightning Network, a second-layer protocol allowing off-chain transactions. Instead of every single transaction being etched into the unyielding stone of the blockchain, the Lightning Network allowed for a series of IOUs to be exchanged between participants, with the final balances being recorded on the blockchain at a later date. IOUs sound a lot like fiat currency... gross.

While the Lightning Network showed promise, it wasn't without its detractors. Critics argued that the system was vulnerable to centralization, as more powerful, well-funded entities could establish themselves as dominant hubs within the network. Other proposed solutions, such as block size increases and sidechains, faced similar challenges and enjoyed varying degrees of success.

The quest for a scalable, secure, and energy-efficient solution continued in the grand cyber dance of digital currency innovation. Newer cryptocurrencies, like Ethereum 2.0, aimed to tackle the scalability issue head-on by transitioning from a PoW model to a Proof-of-Stake (PoS) consensus mechanism, which required users to lock up, or "stake" their tokens as collateral in order to validate transactions.

Ethereum 2.0 was a daring and ambitious plan to shift Ethereum's consensus mechanism, dubbed "The Merge." This metamorphosis promised to reduce energy consumption and increase the network's transaction capacity, making it more accessible to the hordes of developers and users eager to participate in the decentralized revolution.

The transition to Ethereum 2.0 was by no means a simple affair. It was a multi-phase process, beginning with the launch of the Beacon Chain, a separate PoS blockchain that would run parallel to Ethereum's original PoW chain. The plan was to merge the two chains eventually, creating a seamless, unified Ethereum 2.0 network that boasted the best of all worlds: security, energy efficiency, and improved scalability.

However, the journey to Ethereum 2.0 was fraught with peril and risk. The sheer complexity of the upgrade posed a litany of technical obstacles for developers to overcome. Integrating the Beacon Chain with the Ethereum blockchain, known as the "Sharding Phase," was a particularly delicate operation that required careful planning and execution.

Ethereum's metamorphosis also faced a formidable test of trust. The shift from PoW to PoS required Ethereum's vast network of miners, who had invested heavily in mining equipment, to adapt to a new way of validating transactions. This transition held the potential for pushback and resistance from the mining community, who may have felt that their investments were being rendered obsolete.

Moreover, on the PoS consensus mechanism itself, some detractors argued that the new model could inadvertently lead to centralization, as users with larger amounts of Ethereum would wield more influence over the network. This ran counter to the core ethos of decentralization that had inspired the creation of Ethereum and crypto in the first place.

And yet, despite the myriad obstacles, the Ethereum community forged ahead, guided by an unwavering belief in their collective vision of a decentralized (?) future. The Ethereum 2.0 upgrade represented a bold step forward, a leap of faith into the great unknown. It was a testament to the indomitable spirit of human innovation and our relentless pursuit of a better tomorrow.

Spoiler: The fee structure still sucks.

The Problems Created

In the early days of cryptocurrency, the cyber frontier was a wide-open space where transactions zipped through the ether like comets streaking across the night sky. But as more people flocked to the virtual gold rush, the once-spacious expanse began to feel decidedly crowded.

The influx of users strained networks, leading to slower transaction times and skyrocketing fees. The once nimble Bitcoin and Ethereum started to resemble lumbering beasts, struggling to keep up with the rapidly increasing demands of the digital domain.

This congestion had far-reaching consequences for the burgeoning cryptocurrency ecosystem. Users seeking to send or receive crypto found themselves mired in delays and faced with exorbitant fees, diminishing the appeal of cryptocurrencies as a viable alternative to traditional financial systems. For mass adoption to become a reality, something had to change.

Overwhelmed and without catching a breath, another dark cloud appeared on the horizon: the environmental impact of cryptocurrencies. The Proof-of-Work consensus mechanism, underpinning both Bitcoin and the earlier Ethereum, devoured vast quantities of electricity to validate transactions and secure the network.

The staggering energy consumption of PoW mining operations raised eyebrows and pushback from environmentalists and concerned citizens alike. As the world grappled with the urgent need to address climate change and reduce carbon emissions, the energy-intensive nature of PoW cryptocurrencies seemed increasingly at odds with global sustainability efforts.

This tension between the promise of decentralized digital currencies and the environmental cost of their existence added another layer of complexity to the ongoing scalability debate. If cryptocurrencies were to truly take root in the public consciousness and earn widespread acceptance, they would need to find a way to reconcile their innovative potential with their ecological footprint.

On one side of the divide were those who argued that the growing pains experienced by Bitcoin and Ethereum were temporary setbacks, mere obstacles to be overcome in the inexorable march toward progress. They pointed to proposed solutions such as the Lightning Network and Ethereum's transition to Proof-of-Stake as evidence of the cryptocurrency world's adaptability and resilience.

On the other side of the chasm stood those who viewed the scalability problem as an insurmountable hurdle, a fatal flaw that would ultimately doom cryptocurrencies to obscurity and irrelevance. They argued that the environmental impact of PoW, slow transaction times, and high fees associated with network congestion were evidence of crypto's inherent limitations.

And yet, amid the cacophony of discordant voices and competing viewpoints, a harmony emerged: a shared belief in the transformative power of technology and the potential for human ingenuity to chart a path forward.

As the cryptocurrency community grappled with the challenges of scalability and environmental impact, new solutions and innovations continued to arise. From alternative consensus mechanisms like PoS and Delegated Proof-of-Stake (DPoS) to Layer 2 scaling solutions and entirely new blockchain protocols, the race to overcome the limitations of existing digital currencies was in full swing.

In the quest for scalability, Layer 2 solutions emerged as a beacon of hope amid the swirling storm of network congestion. These ingenious innovations sought to ease the burden on the underlying blockchain by offloading transactions to secondary layers or sidechains, allowing for more elegant and efficient transaction processing.

The Lightning Network, as previously mentioned, represented a prime example of a Layer 2 solution, enabling off-chain transactions for Bitcoin that could be settled at a later date. Similarly, Ethereum saw the development of side chains like the Optimistic Rollups and zk-Rollups, which aimed to enhance the network's capacity for processing transactions and smart contracts.

These Layer 2 solutions and sidechains offered a tantalizing glimpse into a future where digital currencies could coexist harmoniously with traditional financial systems; their transactional prowess was no longer hamstrung by the limitations of their underlying blockchain infrastructure.

The challenges faced by the wanderers of the cryptocurrency frontier inspired a new generation of innovators to think outside the proverbial box, giving rise to a cornucopia of specialized blockchain networks. These new networks were designed with specific use cases in mind or crafted to address the limitations of existing systems.

For example, the Polkadot network emerged as a platform focused on facilitating seamless interoperability between different blockchains, allowing them to communicate and transact with one another. Meanwhile, networks like Algorand and Solana were built from the ground up with scalability and high throughput in mind, aiming to address the congestion issues that troubled their predecessors. These novel ideas showcased great potential, but their execution remained rudimentary.

The Solution to the Problems
In the swirling, ever-evolving world of cryptocurrencies and blockchain technology,

keeping up with the latest innovations and contenders vying for supremacy takes time, effort, and a bit of luck. However, in this race, a new player has emerged with the potential to revolutionize the crypto landscape—Kaspa. Developed by a few dedicated experts, Kaspa aims to tackle the persistent issues besetting the likes of Bitcoin and Ethereum while simultaneously pushing the boundaries of what blockchain technology can achieve.

Created with the express purpose of overcoming the limitations of existing cryptocurrencies, Kaspa addresses the problems that have hindered widespread adoption. The developers of Kaspa analyzed the problems plaguing Bitcoin and Ethereum, such as slow transaction speeds, high fees, and energy inefficiency, and set out to create a new network to cure these ailments. In doing so, they have designed a scalable, secure, and environmentally friendly cryptocurrency without sacrificing the core principles of Satoshi Nakamoto and decentralization.

The Blockchain trilemma, as mentioned before, refers to the difficulty of achieving a balance between the three critical components of a blockchain network: decentralization, security, and scalability. Until now, cryptocurrencies have often been forced to prioritize two of these aspects at the expense of the third. Kaspa, however, has found a way to conquer this trilemma, successfully delivering on all three fronts. Through an innovative consensus mechanism, BlockDAG, and the implementation of cutting-edge technology, Kaspa has managed to create a crypto network that is highly decentralized, secure against attacks, and capable of processing a massive number of transactions simultaneously.

As Kaspa continues to gain traction and recognition, it stands poised to usher in a new era of cryptocurrency innovation and adoption. With its groundbreaking solutions to the challenges that have hindered the growth of crypto, Kaspa could potentially become a driving force in the mainstream acceptance of cryptocurrencies. This would not only benefit the entire crypto ecosystem but also serve as a catalyst for further advancements in blockchain technology, empowering developers to continue pushing the envelope and expanding the scope of what is possible. Furthermore, with its open-source ideology, it also encourages the crypto space to model and study from its own tech.

As more and more people begin to understand the advantages of Kaspa and its underlying technology, we may see a shift in public perception of cryptocurrencies. This shift could lead to a greater acceptance of digital currencies as a legitimate form of payment and investment, further solidifying their place in the global financial landscape. In turn, this newfound acceptance could spur a wave of innovation in the fintech and dApp sectors as companies race to develop new products and services that leverage the unique capabilities of cryptocurrencies and blockchain technology.

As the technology behind Kaspa matures and the network becomes increasingly robust, it could attract the attention of major financial institutions and governments alike. This, in turn, could lead to greater integration of cryptocurrencies into the global financial system as more and more businesses and individuals recognize the benefits of using crypto for various transactions. If you can't beat them, make them join you.

The ambitious goals set by the Kaspa developers and its community with their innovative solutions represent a bold and exciting new chapter in cryptocurrencies and blockchain technology. By tackling the issues that have hindered the growth and adoption of Bitcoin and Ethereum, Kaspa has demonstrated its potential to become a game-changer in the realm of finance and economics.

As we look forward to this new era of innovation and adoption, it's essential to remain vigilant and informed. While the promise of a more efficient, secure, and decentralized financial system is undoubtedly alluring, we must maintain sight of the risks and challenges ahead. Only by staying engaged with the latest developments and maintaining a healthy skepticism can we truly appreciate and harness the full potential of Kaspa and other digital currencies that may emerge in the coming years.

If its early success and the dedication of its developers are any indications, Kaspa could set the stage for a financial revolution that transcends the limitations of crypto and fiat currencies. Ultimately, only time will tell if Kaspa can live up to its promise and truly take the crown as the preeminent digital currency in an increasingly interconnected and technologically driven world.

And, as you will discover, time is just another strength of Kaspa's.

Chapter 3

Digital Alchemy

Gather around the digital fire and get ready to burn some s'more NFTs, it's time for a tale about a man named Yonatan Sompolinsky. Picture a young, tall, athletic man with long flowing locks, a penchant for extreme sports, and an insatiable craving for thrill-seeking adventures. Then promptly stop envisioning this person because it's completely wrong.

Yonatan is a computer scientist, crypto addict, and the founder of Kaspa. Fingers dancing across a keyboard, reading, writing, breathing cryptography kind of guy. When Yonatan isn't weaving the threads of the digital future, he's a computer science postdoc at Harvard University. You may recognize his name from something else, however. Ever heard of the Ghost protocol? That was Yonatan's work of art. And it wasn't just some obscure piece of tech stuff. The Ghost protocol got a special mention in the Ethereum whitepaper, which is kind of like getting a shout-out from the Pope at church bingo night. And this is just one of the cool shout-outs of 3316 citations on Google Scholar.

But Yonatan wasn't working solo. He was part of a 2018 supergroup of computer prodigies in a band called DAGlabs, featured on the PolyChain Capital record label. A stadium glam rock band, but replace the guitar solos with algorithms and the screaming fans with lines of code. Shai Wyborski, a quantum and cryptography researcher, was on the keytar. Michael Sutton, a distributed systems researcher and developer, was on drums. Mike Zak, a cryptocurrency and distributed systems developer, handled the bass. Elichai Turkel, a high-performance systems developer, played the lead guitar. And Ori Newman, another cryptocurrency and distributed systems developer, was our frontman. Together, they were the crypto Mötley Crüe behind Kaspa.

So, what's in a name? Well, quite a lot when it comes to this crypto. The word "Kaspa" is ancient Aramaic for both "silver" and "money." This name was selected because of the clear vision for this crypto creation. Kaspa was to be the silver to Bitcoin's gold. Less precious, maybe, but far more practical, usable, and inclusive. Bitcoin was like a golden idol—everyone admired it, but you couldn't exactly use it to buy a cup of coffee.

Pre-Launch

Now, launching a new cryptocurrency without a safety net is like walking a tightrope… well, without a safety net. But for the Kaspa developers, it was more than just a crazy risk. It was a testament to their faith in the project and their belief in the digital currency. They were willing to take that leap of faith, to bet on the strength of their technology and its ideological mission.

An $8,000,000 investment from PolyChain Capital was secured, not just a chunk of change but a vote of confidence in Kaspa's potential and a ticket to ride on a three-year rollercoaster of intense research and development. The Kaspa team used that time to create something genuinely innovative. They didn't take a quick shortcut like forking an existing network; they built an entire cryptocurrency from scratch.

The result? A cryptocurrency embodying the value of all the time, effort, and knowledge in each block, transaction, and line of code.

Kaspa wasn't merely a rehashed Bitcoin or Ethereum version. It was something entirely new, built on a Directed Acyclic Graph (DAG) foundation, a novel architecture distinguishing it from blockchain-based Bitcoin and Ethereum. With this structure and the GHOSTDAG protocol, Kaspa could handle transactions quickly, scalably, decentralized, and energy-efficiently while adhering to a generalized Nakamoto consensus.

The Nakamoto consensus, established by Satoshi Nakamoto, the pseudonymous creator of Bitcoin, states that the longest blockchain—the chain with the most computational work behind it—is the proper chain.

Kaspa takes the original Nakamoto consensus and adapts it. Instead of a single chain, Kaspa applies the principle to the blockDAG.

The GHOSTDAG protocol is crucial in Kaspa's method. It selects the 'blue blocks,' a particular subset of blocks in the DAG. The role of the blue set is to determine the transaction order, allowing multiple blocks to be produced simultaneously without conflicts. Consequently, Kaspa can handle a higher transaction volume.

Creating a revolutionary cryptocurrency like Kaspa is no small feat. It's comparable to inventing a water-run engine. Theoretical and challenging, yet it didn't dissuade the Kaspa developers from dedicating countless hours to development, testing, and fine-tuning.

Central to their algorithm was kHeavyHash, created for a pioneering consensus mechanism known as optical proof-of-work (oPoW), based on the development of optical Application-Specific Integrated Circuits (ASICs). These weren't ordinary ASICs but a revolutionary breed of optical hardware engineered to mine proof-of-work with unmatched energy efficiency. The ultimate goal was to mass-manufacture these optical ASICs, supercharging Kaspa's mining network and leading crypto miners into the next generation.

The initial promise of optical ASICs for greener mining was not fully realized due to the technology's immaturity. Despite this hurdle, Kaspa's kHeavyHash algorithm, initially designed for oPoW, ended up being core-heavy rather than memory-heavy. This unforeseen turn of events became an advantage, as core-heavy processes generate less waste heat, creating a more energy-efficient mining experience.

Even the best entities part ways, and DAGlabs was no exception. The company that had ushered in Kaspa eventually dissolved. Yet Kaspa persevered.

Fair Launch

In the middle of 2021, the decision was taken to suspend funding to the project, primarily because the optical ASICs technology was not yet mature enough for full-scale production. Furthermore, the shift in the cryptocurrency landscape was becoming more noticeable, with declining interest in PoW coins as proof-of-stake networks gained traction. As the November 2021 launch of the mainnet approached, DAGlabs was semi-active, extending part-time support to a handful of developers while waiting for the mainnet to go live.

Once the launch took place, DAGlabs, along with the community, started mining Kaspa. Since almost all of the Polychain initial investment was spent on R&D, the remaining fraction was used for mining activities on rented Amazon hardware.

The coins mined during this period, representing no more than 3% (probably closer to 2.5%) of the maximum supply, were distributed among investors, including Polychain, and former DAGlabs employees and advisors.

Kaspa's decision for a fair launch was a daring move. It showed the universe that Kaspa didn't need the support of venture capitalists, a premine, or a presale. It stood tall, driven by the relentless dedication of its developers and the unwavering backing of its community. This wasn't a quick cash scheme but a long-term commitment to crafting a cryptocurrency that could genuinely make a difference.

DAGlabs officially closed its doors after that, taking some time to dissolve as a legal entity, but its legacy lived on through Kaspa. Despite the odds, Kaspa stood resilient, abiding by the tenacity and innovation that initially sparked its creation.

Kaspa was more than just the product of a tech company. It was the blood, sweat, and brains of a dedicated group of developers and researchers. Working long hours exploring the unknown, uncharted waters on the edge of crypto impossibilities. When they finally cracked the puzzle and solved the unsolvable, they didn't hoard the knowledge and sell it to the highest bidder. Instead, it was handed to the community, given up by people who dreamt, lived, and believed in its potential. Take a moment and let that set in. They gave away the golden goose of crypto. All to the benefit of humanity.

Kaspa operates under an Internet Systems Consortium (ISC) License, a permissive license that lets people do anything with your code with proper attribution and without warranty. The ISC license is functionally equivalent to the BSD 2-Clause and MIT licenses. Meaning that since inception, Kaspa was launched, remains, and will stay completely open source. Kaspa isn't a product. It isn't a rug pull, gimmick, or another useless fringe solution. It's a currency.

Devoid of any central governance or business model, Kaspa is the spirit of the collective in action, a shared belief in the vision and potential of innovative technology to benefit all of humankind.

In the world of Kaspa, everyone has a voice. Its development was a collaborative effort, open to anyone who wanted to contribute. Not just a project for the tech elite, venture capitalists, or a foundation. It was a project for the people, driven by a community that yearns for a fairer, more functional, and more accessible digital currency. You know, like the original goal of Bitcoin and the first cryptocurrencies. Yeah, Kaspa remembered its roots.

When the founding company of the project dissolves, for many projects, it would spell the end. But not for Kaspa. The dissolution of DAGlabs did not mark the demise of Kaspa. Instead, it was a turning point; this scenario was its ideal environment. Kaspa was set free upon the world, like Free Willy but a thousand times better.

The remarkable journey of Kaspa's genesis is a story that highlights the power of innovation, the importance of a supportive community, and the transformative potential of technology. Born out of necessity, forged by a team of experts, and nurtured by a community, Kaspa is a promise of what can be achieved when vision, expertise, and determination come together.

Now, I know what you're thinking with your degen ape brain that works much like my own: "No more history. What do?"

If I had to compare it to something, it's like the Swiss Army Knife of digital currencies. It's a crypto that's packed and primed with unique features, each designed to address the issues inherent in its predecessors, Bitcoin and Ethereum.

To start with, Kaspa is built on a blockDAG architecture. This isn't just a fancy term the developers use to impress their friends at parties or a made-up thing to make the name DAGlabs work. It's a game-changer. Unlike traditional blockchains, the blockDAG allows for the simultaneous processing of blocks. This means quicker confirmations and higher transaction throughput. It's like having a multi-lane highway instead of a single-track dirt road.

It's also more energy efficient. You know how Bitcoin mining is often criticized for consuming more energy than some small countries? Well, Kaspa uses proof-of-work much the same but with a twist. It leverages its DAG structure to reduce the amount of energy needed.

So, you've got a puzzle—a big one, mind you. You've spent hours fitting together the pieces, creating a beautiful portrait of Michael Sutton. Then, suddenly, you find a handful of leftover pieces. They're perfectly good Shai Wyborski pieces, but they clearly don't fit your Michael Sutton puzzle. So, what do you do? Throw them away? It's Shai! Such a waste of a Kaspa collectors-edition puzzle…

That's what Bitcoin does. It throws the Shai pieces away. In the complex cryptographic puzzle that is Bitcoin mining, occasionally, pieces of the puzzle—known as blocks—don't fit into the main blockchain. These are the orphans. In the Bitcoin world, these orphan blocks are discarded, effectively wasting the computational resources that went into creating them.

Now, enter Kaspa and its flashy blockDAG architecture. The brains behind Kaspa looked at these orphan blocks and thought, *How about we stop throwing puzzle pieces away?* And then that's precisely what they did.

In the Kaspa universe, these orphan blocks aren't left out in the cold. Instead, they're brought into the fold, incorporated into the broader network. This approach not only saves computational resources but also boosts the network's overall efficiency. It's like taking those leftover puzzle pieces and creating a brand-new puzzle with them. I guess some kind of super genius Sutton-Wyborski Frankenstein's monster thing. Yep, this analogy has run its course.

The Use Case is Money

So, what's Kaspa used for? Well, due to its scalability and energy efficiency, Kaspa is made for transactions—think buying gas, paying for parking, or even tipping your favorite Kaspa blogger. The low transaction costs and quick confirmation times make it practical for everyday use.

But that's not all. Kaspa is also designed to be a platform for decentralized applications (dApps). Its scalable and efficient architecture makes it an attractive option for developers looking to build the next big thing in the decentralized space. Although layer 2 and smart contracts are in the brainstorming phase, the foundation is planned and built. The layer 2 skyscraper can begin construction anytime.

The big picture is to bring about the next evolution of cryptocurrencies. Kaspa aims to create a digital currency that's not just a store of value or an investment vehicle but a practical tool for daily transactions—actual money; you know, crypto's original dream before it got lost in its forest of deception and useless use cases. It's not about replacing traditional currencies but complementing them, offering a decentralized, efficient, and scalable alternative. Although, it could be a strong contender to replace all currencies.

And the best part is, it's all happening right now. So, HODL onto your monkey pics, degens. The future of cryptocurrencies is here, and its name is Kaspa.

BlockDAG

It's important to note that Kaspa isn't merely a blockchain or a fork of one. It's a different entity altogether. Its secret sauce? You know it, the blockDAG.

Visualize a tree branching out toward the sun, each limb ending with a pomegranate that sprouts another branch, persisting to reach out to the sun without looking back. That tree growth is a directed acyclic graph. The pomegranate is a block in this metaphor, the seeds are transactions, and the sun is the direction of time. The pomegranates are the 'block' in blockDAG.

Unlike Bitcoin or Ethereum, which have a single branch of pomegranates, Kaspa sports a whole network of them. The fascinating part is that although these branches might venture far and wide depending on the demand, the limbs can trace back to a central block or pomegranate while constantly growing toward the sun. This dynamic, ever-evolving ecosystem expands and contracts to meet the network's needs.

Each branch and each pomegranate are part of a larger whole, a cyber tree of interconnected blocks functioning in harmony. The transactions, the seeds within each pomegranate, are essential components and the reason for this tree. Kaspa's elegance lies in this complex yet interconnected structure, making the blockDAG construct revolutionary and efficient.

This blockDAG model brings numerous benefits. Firstly, it allows for the concurrent processing of transactions. While traditional blockchain processes transactions one block at a time, in a blockDAG, several blocks can be processed simultaneously. This results in faster confirmation times and an increased volume of transactions.

Indeed, this structure sounds complicated. But that's where Kaspa's second unique feature, its consensus algorithm, comes into play. Kaspa uses the GHOSTDAG protocol, which functions like a diligent pomegranate farmer sorting out the seeds, ensuring a smooth operation without double-spends or identical seeds.

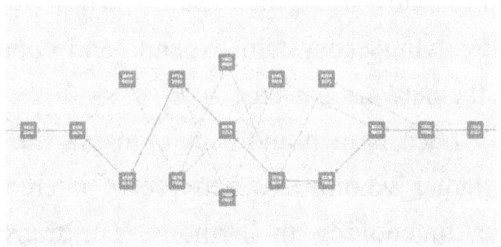

You can watch the blockDAG live and in action here:
kgi.kaspad.net

Everyday Usability

Let's take a moment to appreciate that all this digital dendrology serves a higher purpose. It's not about building a faster, more efficient, more complex cryptocurrency for its own sake. Instead, it's about addressing real-world challenges, making cryptocurrency a practical tool for everyday transactions instead of just a speculative asset.

Kaspa's blockDAG model provides scalability, a substantial problem with cryptocurrencies today. As more people use Kaspa, the system won't become bogged down, just as a tree growing into the open sky doesn't slow down or stop growth due to an overhead canopy.

Let's consider its practical applications beyond Kaspa's origin story, technology, and mission. We're not sending a rocket to the moon; we're discussing a cryptocurrency intended for use here on Earth. However, if we liken Kaspa to a rocket, it's just cleared the launch pad, and the trajectory is promising.

I won't bombard you with statistics. We've all seen enough bar graphs and pie charts to last a lifetime. It's worth noting that Kaspa's adoption rate among both institutions and individuals is growing exponentially. And this isn't limited to fringe applications. We're talking about everyday transactions—buying a burger, paying for a hotel, trading on exchanges. Remember when I mentioned that Kaspa was designed for practical daily transactions? Well, it's living up to that promise and is doing so now.

What's driving this adoption? Partly, it's Kaspa's unique features—speed, scalability, decentralization, and energy efficiency. But another significant factor is the integrations and community.

Kaspa isn't a lone wolf. It's more like a social butterfly wolf, say Wolf9466, but instead of talking tech, it's winning over organizations, businesses, and projects for integration. These users expand Kaspa's reach, opening up new avenues of use and connecting different aspects of the ecosystem.

Each integration is mutually beneficial. Kaspa reaches new user bases, and the integrator leverages Kaspa's unique features. It's akin to a band collaborating with a famous singer for a song—the band gets more exposure, and the singer experiments with a new sound.

The heart of Kaspa isn't just the technology, it's the community. In Kaspa's world, there's no central authority. Instead, decisions are made collectively by the users. This democratic approach means that Kaspa isn't just a cryptocurrency; it's an experiment in collective decision-making.

Kaspa is community-driven, and its members determine its development direction. This ensures that Kaspa remains decentralized, relevant, and in tune with its users' needs and aspirations.

Along with community governance, Kaspa is also community funded. This isn't just a fancy way of saying 'crowdfunding'; it's about being a stakeholder, not for financial gain but for contributing time, energy, and expertise.

So, Kaspa is more than just a piece of cutting-edge technology. It's a collective project that brings people together, pooling resources and working toward a common goal. It's community governance, a shared mission, and mutual growth.

Kaspa's Future

Looking toward the horizon, the contributors behind Kaspa are continually refining and upgrading the system. Kaspa is adapting the Rustlang rewrite, known for speed, reliability, and memory safety, enhancing the network's performance.

Then there's DAG KNIGHT, a protocol upgrade, making Kaspa the world's first parameterless cryptocurrency. It allows the network to self-adjust to network health and latency, rendering it more efficient.

Layer 2 is planned, expanding capacity without compromising the existing structure. This will allow Kaspa to handle more transactions, unique functions, and operate at an even higher efficiency level.

The introduction of Smart Contracts will empower users to automate transactions and create permissionless operations, making every Kaspa user a creator.

Kaspa's journey is still being written, and every member of the Kaspa community is an author. This story is for everyone, from the business owner looking for a faster, cheaper way to process transactions to the everyday person who wants to avoid waiting in lines for food to the blogger contributing their part to a community changing the world.

Chapter 4

PHANTOMSs and GHOSTs and DAGs, Oh My!

Well, here we are. You've caught me mid-insomnia, not driven by the fear of mangling this chapter, which is a distinct possibility, but from the weight of demystifying the arcane texts of the PHANTOM GHOSTDAG. Written by the sagacious triad: Yonatan Sompolinsky, Shai Wyborski, and Aviv Zohar. These great minds in cryptography have spent countless hours and much mental prowess crafting this protocol.

The decision to write about PHANTOM GHOSTDAG isn't just some idea that popped into my head one sunny afternoon while sipping tea. No, it's more like a beast that's been gnawing at my leg, a 'SPECTRE' that's haunting my dreams. This protocol has been wrestled into existence through a gauntlet of academics, forged in the fires of cryptography, and refined by the dogged determination to eat, breathe, and sleep

GHOSTDAG. That's a tough act to follow, very tough indeed.

I'm not trying to exaggerate, but the sheer magnitude of effort and knowledge injected into the PHANTOM GHOSTDAG is nothing short of staggering, and I'll be the first to admit, I doubt I can do it justice. The effort to fully comprehend this monumental task feels like attempting to land a hole-in-one in golf on your first swing. It's just not happening, at least not how I play.

But you know what? I'm going to give it a whirl. Because you, dear reader, should understand just how much work has gone into this protocol. You deserve to appreciate the scale of this undertaking and the immense commitment that has driven it. So, bear with me as I dive into the labyrinth of intricacies of the PHANTOM GHOSTDAG and try to unravel its complexities for you. Worst-case scenario, we hold each other while we wait for the consensus minotaur to find us.

Without further ado, YOLO!

Dogs and DAGs

So, what exactly is this "Phantom ghost dog?" What flavor of Scooby-Snack is this mystery all about? Well, it's a far cry from meddling kids and villains masquerading as monsters. It's a protocol that's not only upending blockchain technology as we know it but also setting the stage for a more exciting, cutting-edge, and sophisticated future. One that is so advanced that previous cryptocurrencies could only dream of it. But before we delve into the complexities of PHANTOM GHOSTDAG, we need to take a step back and talk about its predecessor—the Nakamoto Consensus.

So, back to the mysterious Satoshi Nakamoto, the unidentified individual or group, or maybe even Yonatan, who brought us Bitcoin. Nakamoto didn't just create a new form of digital currency but also built the foundation on which all blockchain technology rests: the Nakamoto Consensus. It's the backbone of blockchain, the cornerstone of cryptocurrency. Understanding this protocol is critical to appreciating the groundbreaking innovations of the PHANTOM GHOSTDAG.

The General Consensus

Let's take a trip back in time, a little bit further in the past than 2009, straight to the heart of the Byzantine Empire. Here's the scenario: a group of Byzantine generals, each commanding a retinue of the mighty Byzantine army. Success in battle is hanging by a thread that requires impeccably coordinated battle plans. But there's a snag. Communication between the generals is as unreliable as second-hand armor, limited to messengers who may or may not reach their destination. And just to stir the pot a bit more, some of these generals may be traitors.

To succeed, every general must agree on attacking or retreating in unison. If one general fails to do as the others, they will all perish in medieval fashion. So, the question is burning on everyone's mind: How can the trusted generals coordinate to ensure that every general receives the correct message, given the risks of lost messages and misinformation from traitors? Welcome to the Byzantine General Problem.

Fast forward to our contemporary, somewhat more civilized, digital era, where the battlefield of the blockchain world mirrors the Byzantine predicament. Here, the generals are nodes or miners within the blockchain network, and the battle plans are transactions that need to be added to the blockchain. The traitors? They're potential fraudulent transactions, attackers, and attempts at double-spending.

The Nakamoto Consensus plays a critical role here and is our story's knight in shining armor. It prevents the traitors, or fraudulent transactions, from wreaking havoc by ensuring that each transaction is validated by a majority of nodes. This process, my friends, is known as proof-of-work.

Imagine you're watching a race where miners compete to solve complex mathematical puzzles, their eyes on the prize: the chance to add blocks to the blockchain. Each solved puzzle adds a link or block to the chain, creating a ledger of transactions. But here's the twist. The longest chain—the one representing the most accumulated computational work—is the winner. It's the chain accepted by the network as the valid ledger of transactions. This longest-chain rule is the core of the Nakamoto Consensus, providing a robust and reliable foundation for decentralized transactions.

Equipped with the knowledge of the Nakamoto Consensus and the Byzantine General Problem, we can now explore the intricate and fascinating structure of PHANTOM GHOSTDAG.

A Protocol Puzzle

My first introduction to the PHANTOM GHOSTDAG was much like my initial encounter with a Rubik's cube—I was puzzled, intrigued, and mostly overwhelmed. But as with any other enigma, the satisfaction of comprehending the details is gratifying. PHANTOM GHOSTDAG is a protocol that could transform how we think about blockchain. And it will, since Kaspa is a blockDAG and not a blockchain.

Blockchain has always been fascinating. The idea of a decentralized, unalterable ledger of information was revolutionary when it first surfaced. Bitcoin made this idea mainstream, but the technology behind it held promise for so much more. However, as Bitcoin's popularity grew, the limitations of its original protocol, Nakamoto Consensus, became more apparent, especially in areas like scalability and transaction speed.

This is where PHANTOM GHOSTDAG comes in. GHOSTDAG stands for Greedy Heaviest Observed SubTree Directed Acyclic Graph. A mouthful, I know, but stick with me. This protocol aims to rectify those nagging Nakamoto Consensus issues. It's like the next-gen upgrade of the original blockchain protocol. But here's the catch: it's extraordinarily complex, like solving not one but a dozen Rubik's cubes simultaneously and at an incredibly rapid pace.

Picture a traditional blockchain like a one-lane country road with one of those old-fashioned toll booths right smack in the middle. Each car—or "block"—waits its turn to pass through, its information recorded in the ledger by the attendant, let's call him Bape. It's a straightforward, orderly queue, but it's got the speed of downloading a copy of Myst Masterpiece Edition on dialup.

Now, instead of that back road, I want you to think about the autobahn. That's PHANTOM GHOSTDAG for you. Think eighteen lanes of unrestricted, pedal-to-the-metal speed. Cars here, there, everywhere. Each represents a block, racing past the toll booth like the Indy 500. And remember Bape, the toll booth guy? His job's just gotten a heck of a lot more interesting.

You see, Bape isn't just scribbling down entries in a straight line anymore. Instead, he has a giant sketch pad, jotting down each car and drawing lines between them to show who arrived and where and from which direction. He's even referencing the myriad cars before them because that's how Bape rolls, like an over-stimulated tollbooth conspiracist that's seen too many detective shows. The combination of Bape and the highway is the essence of the blockDAG structure. It allows blocks to be added in relation to numerous others, not just the one before it, seriously revving up the speed at which transactions, the passengers inside the cars, can be processed.

This isn't your grandma's Bitcoin transaction processing. This is the autobahn—it's faster, more efficient, and highly motivated to get from point A to point B. That, my friend, is the power of PHANTOM GHOSTDAG.

Now, if you're thinking, "Okay, that sounds great, but what about security?" Of course, an essential aspect of blockchain technology is its ability to ensure the integrity and security of data. This is where the PHANTOM part of the PHANTOM GHOSTDAG comes into play.

PHANTOM is a protocol that adds a layer of security to the GHOSTDAG structure. It uses a unique system to select the DAG's main chain and resolve conflicts. When you allow blocks to be added concurrently, you open the door to conflicts. For example, two blocks might contain conflicting transactions, and we need a way to decide which one is valid. This is where the Nakamoto Consensus struggles. It just can't handle these conflicts efficiently.

PHANTOM colorfully tackles this problem. It selects the main chain based on a 'coloring' algorithm, marking blocks as either blue (valid) or red (invalid). The algorithm determines which blocks to color blue based on the weight of their references to previous blocks, with heavier blocks getting preference. Weight generally refers to the cumulative measure of support that a block has from other blocks in the network. This support is typically determined by the number of direct and indirect references a block has from other blocks added after it.

When a new block is created, it references previous blocks. Each reference increases the 'weight' of the referenced block. Blocks with more connections from other blocks are considered "heavier" or of higher weight. It's a bit like choosing which of two conflicting stories to believe based on the credibility of their sources.

This might sound complicated. Well, that's because it is. The PHANTOM GHOSTDAG protocol takes the original blockchain concept and adds several layers of complexity to it. However, the potential benefits are tremendous. It represents a significant leap forward in the evolution of blockchain technology, with the potential to handle a far greater volume of transactions and provide even greater security than existing protocols.

Burst Blocks

One aspect that makes PHANTOM GHOSTDAG intriguing is the concept of a 'burst.' In the protocol's language, a 'burst' refers to an event where the honest network produces a chain of blocks and the adversary creates none. This term also refers to the blocks made during the event known as 'burst blocks.' I don't know about you, but the Starburst fruity taffy candy immediately comes to mind. I could go for some tropical Starburst blocks right now.

In a decentralized network like a blockchain, you must always account for the bad guys. These adversaries might try to disrupt the system or create fraudulent transactions. PHANTOM GHOSTDAG has a unique way of dealing with this.

The protocol's design assures that the honest network won't be easily duped by a block from a deceptive chain that lacks any burst blocks. To simplify it, imagine it like this: the network has a built-in 'lie detector' that can identify the integrity of incoming blocks. If there's no truth (burst blocks) within the claim (the new block), the lie detector flags it. This mechanism is critical in upholding the system's integrity.

However, just like any lie detector in the real world, PHANTOM GHOSTDAG's protocol isn't perfect. There is a certain chance, albeit small, that the honest network might be fooled by a block without any burst blocks. This probability is influenced by the system parameters and always has a positive lower bound. This means there's always a slight risk of being fooled, but the system comes prepared with an extra spare tire, a can of gas, and a packet of astronaut ice cream in the trunk.

Another security feature are these things called "hourglass blocks." Despite the name, they have nothing to do with the sands of time or some cryptic life metaphor. Instead, think of them as the bouncers and DJs at an all-night music festival. These ambassadors of rock 'n' roll keep the party pumping and the roof raising.

At this epic bash, everyone's invited to contribute to the playlist with their favorite album. But here's the catch—no duplicate albums are allowed. House rules. We want a unique, diverse soundtrack for our party, reflecting the tastes of all attendees.

So, who ensures this melodic harmony? Enter the hourglass blocks. Imagine them as an automated DJ system, balancing the tunes and setting the party mood. They're not quite as personable as Jimbo, our Telegram admin. Still, they're consistent and fair, spinning the records with a robot DJ's precision.

Here's how it grooves: Two guests, Tim and Josh, both bring the same Beatles album. Tim's album hit the DJ booth first, but there's more buzz for Josh's copy of the same record. The hourglass block, our automated DJ, evaluates both the arrival order and the crowd's anticipation. Considering these factors, it decides to spin Josh's record. Sorry, Tim, but MC Hourglass has dropped the mic.

But hold up, there's a twist in our party plot. Trickster Tiram tries to game the system by smuggling in multiple copies of his Polka album, hoping to flood the playlist. Well, the hourglass blocks aren't easily fooled. They're designed to prevent such disruptive moves. So, even if Trickster Tiram submits his unpopular Polka album multiple times, the system ensures a balanced representation of all the party-goers' musical preferences.

Translating this back into blockDAG speak, each guest represents a node in the network, and the albums they bring symbolize the blocks of transactions they propose. PHANTOM

GHOSTDAG, through its hourglass blocks, prevents any single node from dominating the transaction history (like Trickster Tiram's Polka overload). Instead, it ensures that the order of transactions is fair and representative of the network's broader activity, leading to a harmonious blockchain "party."

So, what happens if an adversary still manages to create a fraudulent block? Well, that's where the PHANTOM GHOSTDAG's advanced security measures come into play.

Suppose an adversary creates a block that doesn't reference any burst blocks and tries to sweet-talk the network to accept it. In that case, they're starting a block race with a disadvantage. In other words, they're trying to win a marathon while starting a few miles behind everyone else. Not impossible but not easy.

This race is where hourglass blocks come into play—they're the runners with Nike Shox that keep the honest runners' pace steady. The adversary's pace fluctuates wildly and has to somehow outperform and fight through the stampede of hourglass blocks. This inherent advantage of the honest network helps ensure the security and integrity of the blockchain. So, next time you're participating in a running of the bulls, try an erratic pace and see how that works out for you.

Want to taste the spectral rainbow? Similar to previous conflicted transactions, PHANTOM GHOSTDAG's coloring algorithm steps in to referee when there's a conflict between blocks. It considers the weight of a block's references and the overall structure of the DAG to determine which block should be marked blue and which should be marked red. A unique take on color by numbers.

It might seem a bit abstract, but think about it this way: It's like a high-tech version of the children's game "Telephone." If you've got a line of kids passing along a message, the message can get distorted along the way. The coloring algorithm is the diligent teacher who steps in, listens to the original message and the current version, and makes a judgment call about which is more accurate.

So, how will all this advanced tech revolutionize the financial world? Well, you know those bank lines? The dreary wait while each transaction is processed one by one teller? Kiss those goodbye with PHANTOM GHOSTDAG. It's like walking into a bank and seeing dozens of tellers, all ready to handle your transactions in parallel. The speed? Unprecedented. The efficiency? Off the charts. The middleman? Yeah, not needed. It's the future of finance at your fingertips. You can be your own bank.

Now, let's talk about digital currencies. They're not just for tech geeks anymore. With PHANTOM GHOSTDAG, cryptocurrencies have become much more feasible for everyday use. Your morning coffee, weekly grocery haul, and monthly bills could be paid seamlessly and instantaneously using digital currency. A world where digital currencies are as commonplace as cash or credit, with no lines!

And then there are the big financial institutions. You know, the folks who move money around the world like chess pieces. For them, PHANTOM GHOSTDAG could be like adding a turbo-boost to their operations. With its ability to handle high volumes of transactions quickly and securely, it could streamline processes, improve security, and potentially save a truckload of money. That's no small change, believe me.

But let's not forget about commerce. Online shopping, for instance, could get a massive boost from PHANTOM GHOSTDAG. With faster, secure transaction processing, you could click 'buy' one second and receive your purchase confirmation the next. It's like upgrading from snail mail to instant messaging.

You get all these speeds, scalability, security, and decentralization benefits. Many cryptocurrencies claim the same, but Kaspa and its PHANTOM GHOSTDAG don't make claims. It offers a solution without any sacrifice.

Looking back at the big picture, it's clear that the PHANTOM GHOSTDAG protocol represents a significant evolution in blockchain technology. Its unique combination of scalability and advanced security measures could revolutionize the world of decentralized networks.

Of course, as with any groundbreaking technology, it's not without challenges; the complexity of the PHANTOM GHOSTDAG protocol makes it a tough nut to crack. But as we've seen time and time again, the tech world loves a good challenge. And who knows? Perhaps one day, we'll look back at PHANTOM GHOSTDAG the same way we look back at the original blockchain—as a revolutionary step forward that paved the way for a whole new world of possibilities. This might happen sooner than you think… more on that later.

Block Magic

That's a glimpse into the complex but intriguing world of PHANTOM GHOSTDAG. I know it's a lot to digest; however, I hope this deep dive has shed some light on this exciting protocol. It demonstrates the innovative spirit of the tech world and our insatiable appetite for progress. And though it might seem daunting now, remember the words of Arthur C. Clarke, "Any sufficiently advanced technology is indistinguishable from magic." PHANTOM GHOSTDAG may be more mystical and spectral than magical. Still, I hope that I have helped demystify this technological specter.

PHANTOM GHOSTDAG is a complex beast, no doubt about it. But its potential is enormous. It seeks to address some of the most significant challenges facing blockchain today, namely the blockchain trilemma. Achieving scalability, security, and decentralization without sacrifices. This is a considerable accomplishment in a world where digital transactions are becoming increasingly important. They are the keys to a more efficient, more secure digital future.

And remember, the complexity of PHANTOM GHOSTDAG isn't a bug; it's a feature. It allows the protocol to operate with the level of sophistication necessary to meet the demands of a global digital economy. As with all things complex, it requires patience, understanding, and a willingness to grapple with the intricacies of its design.

Chapter 5

The Heartbeat is Community Governance

Having melted our cerebral circuits trying to decrypt the enigmatic enigma that is PHANTOM GHOSTDAG. It's time we took a respite from the torrent of tech terminology like 'blockDAG,' 'trilemma,' and 'Starbursts.' Yes, Kaspa's engine room is a technological marvel, but the definitive power source driving this network isn't just advanced code—it's us, the dwellers of the ordinary world. That's right—you, me, and even the fortunate folks pocketing KAS. But let's zoom in on those unafraid to strain their hands with cramps from typing.

Venturing into the digital agora that is Kaspa is like getting sucked into a tornado and feeling like you're not in Kansas anymore. And it's no dull affair. Instead, it vibrates with life, incessantly busy with tasks that ebb and flow, priorities in flux, and a relentless stream of information. Picture a party that defies the hands of time, a diverse congregation of technomancers, business savants, wide-eyed visionaries, champion wordsmiths, and spirited greenhorns. Everyone here has their unique narrative, yet they're all tethered together by a shared foresight—a unified Kaspa dream of what exists today and what tomorrow may bring.

Kaspa isn't some high-tech fortress ruled by the few. There's no formal foundation, no hierarchical team, and definitely no venture capitalists calling the shots. It's more like a digital town square where everyone's voice matters. It's a place where opinions are heard, votes are counted, and decisions are made collectively. It's a democratic republic floating soundly in the ocean of crypto. Kaspa: where the community sets the course and charts the future of finance.

At the heart of this bustling operation is good ol' voting—the ancient system that is simple, direct, and as baseline as it gets. An online congregation where souls from every corner of the globe convene, their voices resonating, sparking debates, and shaping the very course of Kaspa's destiny. It's democracy in its purest form, thriving amidst this cyber hub's lively hustle and bustle.

And here's the fascinating part: nothing is off-limits regarding these governance discussions. From significant network upgrades that make seasoned tech junkies break a sweat to seemingly trivial tasks like tweaking the logo, everything is subject to be thrown into the ring for debate, advocacy, and a communal vote. And you know who's in command? The regular folks like you and me, without borders or biases, voicing our opinions in a global Kaspa conference call.

And when decision time arrives, it's like the grand finale of a talent show. Ideas compete for the audience's favor, and the best ones rise to the top like bubbles in a fizzy algorithmic soda. There's suspense, excitement, and a few sweaty palms as people eagerly await the results. Which idea will take center stage? Only discussion, time, and the whims of the voting gods will tell.

So, what's the secret ingredient that keeps this wild governance saloon running? Camaraderie. It's where friendships are forged through late-night discussions, between rounds of CS:GO, and the shared passion for Pepsi Max. It's a group of globally scattered friends where collaborations bloom like virtual tulips, and support is as abundant as Spiderman memes on the internet. It's a place where you can find your digital tribe, a crew of like-minded adventurers ready to explore the boundless possibilities of Kaspa.

And speaking of exploration, this crew isn't satisfied with just sailing familiar seas. They have an insatiable appetite for the new, the improved, and the cutting-edge. They thrive on breaking molds, trailblazing, and venturing into uncharted territory.

Take the Rusty Kaspa transformation, for example. It's a tale for the history books. The community looked at Golang—the programming language that gave life to the Kaspa network—and thought, "Hey, why not revamp the whole codebase from scratch?" And they freaking did! Those crazy devs. Anyway, with their sights on Rustlang, a language focused on security, performance, and memory management; it's like swapping your old Honda Accord for a shiny, sleek, new Lambo. Rust brings guarantees against bugs and a powerful type system that would make any data structure swoon. So, collectively, they decided to give their fancy, relatively new network a fresh coat of Rust.

Now, you might be wondering, how does a seemingly crazy idea like revamping an entire network come about? Well, it can start anywhere, really. These social gatherings are buzzing with discussions and activities on Twitter, Reddit, and

Telegram. And if an idea catches fire outside of Discord, you can bet it will make its way there eventually.

The Heart of the Community

Discord is really where the magic happens. A Mos Eisley cantina of the internet, just without the aliens that shoot first and much fewer lightsaber duels. In the #general-channel and specialized channels, you'll find the pulse of Kaspa, where community members are passionate about discussing, sharing perspectives, and shaping the path forward. It's where the initial seeds of inspiration find fertile ground and sprout into remarkable projects.

After all the debates, discussions, and questions, if an idea gains acceptance, it moves on to the stage of proposals. This is where you stand on your virtual soapbox, deliver a passionate spiel about your concept, and then, in a truly democratic fashion, leave its fate to a vote. If it gets a thumbs-down, don't fret—it's just the universe's way of telling you that your idea needs a bit of polishing. So, pour yourself a big mug of creativity juice (coffee, for the uninitiated) and get back at it.

But if the proposal weathers the storm and emerges victorious, cue the Rocky theme song! A polished draft is presented for a final vote in the formal #votes-channel. This is where the actual decision-making happens. The voting usually lasts about 24 hours, but it may run longer if it's a doozy to ensure everyone has their say. Flexibility and adaptability are key here, like a contortionist at a yoga retreat.

If the vote is in favor, it's time to get down to business. The moderators broadcast a crowdfunding call-to-arms in the #funding-pools channel. They'll lay out the mission specifics, the bounty details, the funding duration, and a contingency plan in case the funding falls short. In some cases, if the crowdfund isn't asking for the moon and the members are chomping at the bit, they might bypass the vote and get on with it.

Crowdfunds are the Kaspa way of community funding, a donation-based wellspring of opportunity for groundbreaking projects, innovative developments, and community-driven initiatives. They are the lifeblood of Kaspa's evolution, offering a means to fund ambitious undertakings that propel this digital universe forward. Whether it's revamping the entire network's codebase, exploring new consensus mechanisms, securing listings or integrations, or fueling marketing campaigns that ignite curiosity and adoption, the possibilities are vast.

Most crowdfunds end up in the unified Kaspa public development fund, a multi-sig wallet where the treasurers hold the keys. It's like a digital treasure chest guarded by demisrael, msutton, TheSheepCat, and Tim. They didn't choose the treasurer life; the treasurer life chose them, probably by a Discord vote. The crowdfunds are separated by addresses in this wallet to avoid any unseemly mix-ups.

The epic quest for 100M KAS to rewrite the Kaspa codebase in Rust, was one crowdfund that had everyone on the edge of their seats. It required a special vault, a multi-sig 3/6 wallet manned by the Rust Committee, elected by vote. Then, another crowdfunding drive was needed for 70M Kaspa for the DAG KNIGHT protocol. Same vault, different compartment. Talk about high-stakes adventures.

Once the loot is in the proposer's hands, they're the sole party responsible for managing the funds. Typically, milestones are set for the development process and, either way, approved by the community as part of the proposal. But if you're curious about the coin's journey, you can always track it through the Kaspa Explorer. Just don't expect any treasure maps.

In one remarkable tale of mass collaboration, the determined fellows embarked on a crowdfunding mission to secure a listing for their unique blockchain-based project on Gate.io. Their goal? To raise $50,000 in KAS and an additional $50,000 in USDT. This collective effort attracted diverse participants, each contributing their own crypto assets, marketing strategies, and words of encouragement. The overwhelming support demonstrated once again the incredible capacity of this society to achieve the seemingly unachievable.

With the funds securely in hand, Gate.io stepped up to the plate, allocating $50,000 to a full-blown marketing campaign. They saw this opportunity for greatness and wanted to create an unforgettable listing experience for their users. It was a veritable two-for-one victory—the Kaspa community not only secured their coveted listing but also landed a kickass marketing campaign to boot. That's not just a win. That, my friends, is worthy of its own 80s montage.

Kaspa isn't just reactive; they're always a step ahead, devising, plotting, and ready for the next leap. You've witnessed the prowess of developers who work tirelessly behind the scenes with their brilliant minds like cyborg supercomputers. They dedicate more time to lines of code than to breathing, fix bugs, introduce new features, and keep Kaspa running faster than a cracked out hamster on an escape trajectory from its wheel.

But here's the deal, amid all this tech jibber-jabber, it's vital to remember that the Kaspa macrocosm isn't just made up of blinking servers, intricate algorithms, and a parade of innovative applications. Sure, those are undeniably cool, like owning a DeLorean cool, but they're not the heart of the story. The real deal is the dynamic bunch of users and members who bridge the chasm between the indecipherable lines of code and the avalanche of tech lingo.

Are Thou Worthy?

To solidify just how vital community governance is, even the brainiest of proposals from our revered core developers don't just waltz into the Kaspa world unopposed. Oh no, they, too, must withstand the trials of public opinion. No matter its origin, every idea must earn its place under the Kaspa sun. Each proposal goes through the same rigorous voting process. Only the worthiest ideas survive.

And if you thought Kaspa was only for those immersed in the mystic arts of proposals, politics, and code, think again! There are many ways to get involved and dive into this bustling metropolis. Moderators, translators, marketers, traders, miners, and businesses make up the functional elements of a government that genuinely works for its people. Kaspa is a multifaceted neighborhood that thrives on diversity, with roles more varied than pizza toppings. Unless it's pineapple, we have no room for you pineapple people.

The Contributing Members
Now, let's shine the spotlight on the masked, caped moderators standing on the rooftops of Kaspa City, their keyboards glistening in the moonlight. With an uncanny sixth sense, they sniff out trouble and swoop in like caped crusaders, ensuring that Kaspa remains a respectful and inclusive environment for all. They listen to everyone's voices, make decisions that benefit the entire community, and maintain order with their trusty keyboards, acting as the Batman and Wonder Woman of social management. They're the heroes we need to keep a harmonious digital environment.

The community helpers are the friendly folks armed with endless knowledge and hearts of gold. They're like the beloved grandmas and grandpas of the neighborhood, always ready to share their wisdom and lend a helping hand. Whether you need assistance with a coding problem or guidance with running a node, they've got your back, guiding you through the virtual landscape with a dash of humor and a genuine desire to support. These helpers spread kindness and knowledge throughout the social media platforms, making it a warm and welcoming place.

Then there are the linguistic experts, not to be confused with linguini experts—the translators—who bring Kaspa's wonders to the world. With their impressive language skills, they break down language barriers, transforming the platform's content, documents, and user interfaces into languages spoken by people from all walks of life. It's as if they possess a magic wand that makes words universally understood. Expecto Localizationum! Could use that mastery of basic English myself.

And then we have the business and marketing professionals—the smooth talkers and hype generators of the Kaspa cosmos. Armed with creativity and an uncanny ability to grab attention, they craft ingenious strategies, conduct market research, and launch campaigns that make Kaspa the talk of the town. They sprinkle that marketing magic dust, attracting new users, devising accessibility plans, and making Kaspa shine brighter than a disco ball at a lively rave. They are the masters of hype, the maestros of marketing, and at the time of writing, rubarbarian brought the Community Marketing Fund (CMF) into existence, which has become a powerhouse for driving community engagement and adoption. It's like a perpetual motion machine for marketing campaigns, contributor incentives, and brand merchandise.

In this vibrant ecosystem of governance entities, the admins take on the role of overseers, aiding in coordinating developers, moderators, helpers, translators, and business and marketing professionals. Don't mistake these folks for the stereotypical dictators you might imagine from your school group projects. Instead, the admins are more like the steadfast conductors of a digital symphony. They've mastered the art of working in harmony with a medley of talents to create a masterpiece of decentralized governance. These folks are the squad of core contributors who've earned their stripes through blood, sweat, and code.

Imagine a constantly changing society where boundaries are relentlessly pushed and laurels are left untouched. This crew of passionate individuals continually creates, shapes, innovates, and redefines what a crypto community can be. The spirit of Kaspa extends far beyond the present—it's about embracing the future and its endless possibilities. A thrilling plunge into the unknown, embarking on an adventure that knows no bounds in the vast virtual realm. The energy, ambition, and vision are simply magnetic, drawing in individuals from all backgrounds and skill sets and weaving them into the vibrant tapestry of Kaspa.

As I sit here, penning these words, I can envision Kaspa community members scattered across the globe, huddled over their keyboards and lost in a world of ideas and possibilities. They toil away, fueled by passion, curiosity, and determination, in different time zones, under other skies and different stars, united by their shared purpose. They're not simply tinkering with the fate of Kaspa—they're reshaping the entire landscape of digital currencies. Together, they're authoring a new chapter in the book of tech innovation, one that's destined to become a standard model for other digital tribes out there.

So, how does someone like yourself get involved? It's simple, really. All you have to do is open your mouth and start talking. Yep, that's right—voicing your thoughts, ideas, and opinions is the first step to becoming a part of this dynamic universe. Jump into the lively discussions happening on social media platforms like Twitter, Reddit, and Telegram. You'll find yourself in a swirling vortex of ideas and perspectives spanning languages and biomes. Don't be shy; join the conversation and be heard.

If you like what you see and hear and want to take your participation to the next level, consider volunteering for a role within the community. Become a helper, offering your expertise and knowledge to assist others. Need help with coding? Node setup? Wallet troubleshooting? (Find the legendary sa1krishna Discord, but don't tell him I sent you) You name it—there's always someone who could use a helping hand. Be an advocate, spreading kindness, humor, and knowledge like confetti at a digital parade. Maybe even write a book like some kind of sociopath.

And hey, if you're more of a developer, this is your playground! Kaspa welcomes brilliant minds like yours to join the ranks of the code warriors. Tinker, create and innovate code, troubleshoot, and introduce mind-blowing features. You're like a digital wizard, conjuring magic with every keystroke. So, roll up your sleeves, fire up your favorite coding language, and let your creativity run wild. Once the Rust codebase is complete, Layer 2 and smart contracts will be waiting around the corner. Now is the time to be a part of that brainstorming. Together, we'll build a digital empire that's the envy of the tech world.

Outreach

Now, let's talk marketing, baby! Are you a smooth talker? A master of hype and persuasion? Then the world of Kaspa needs your skills. Dive into business and marketing, crafting strategies, conducting market research, and launching campaigns that'll make Kaspa the talk of the town. You're the maestro of excitement, the conductor of curiosity, and the spokesperson of all things Kaspa.

Along with the CMF, the marketers and translators are ushering in ambassadors, too! A perfect mix of global outreach and another opportunity to watch for. Focused on regional education and inclusion, ambassadors will be a Kaspa conduit for their language areas. So, get ready to sprinkle that marketing magic dust and bring in new users while making Kaspa shine.

However, you don't have to be a developer or a marketing guru to make an impact. Just by using Kaspa, you're already contributing to the community. Every transaction and every interaction with the network adds to the vitality and growth of this digital ecosystem. So go ahead, send and receive KAS, explore the possibilities, and let your usage display the practical power of Kaspa.

My Beginnings

Looking back to my own humble beginnings. Amidst the Ethereum merge, I was just your average Joe, marveling at the spectacle of crypto history being etched right before my eyes. I stumbled upon Kaspa, and, man, that KGI visualizer had me hooked. I wanted to dig deeper, but lo and behold, no Medium posts. It was like attempting to assemble IKEA furniture without the instruction manual—it wasn't coming together in my brain. So, in a fit of curiosity-induced frustration, I asked Tim, "Medium?" And then, shortly after I found out one needed to be made, I started the Kaspa Currency Medium. And now, well, I'm still your average Joe, who sometimes scribbles away about Kaspa.

Your Beginnings

There's a place for everyone in this wild and wonderful construct of Kaspa community governance. Whether you're a talker, a helper, a developer, a marketer, or simply a user, your unique talents and perspectives are valued. So, jump in, take action, and join us on this exhilarating adventure. Together, we'll redefine what it means to be a collective, and together, we'll create a legacy that'll make the digital world stand up and take notice. Welcome to the Kaspa family—let's make history, set the future, and have some fun while changing the world!

Chapter 6

The Tokenomics and the Miners

It's always about the damn numbers, isn't it? Those little devils with their absolute, unchanging truth. They're like the divas of the mathematical world, strutting around, flaunting their elegance and complexity. They hold the power to shape our lives, reveal the secrets of the universe, and tell us when things won't work just to mess with our heads.

Take zero, for instance. Can you believe ancient Indian mathematicians didn't even consider it a number until the 7th century AD? It's like they were living in a numerical dark age, utterly oblivious to the existence of nothingness. Imagine their surprise when they finally discovered the joy of factoring in one more number when counting to infinity. It was probably the mathematical equivalent of inventing fire or finding out that Tim's airdrop isn't actually real.

And let's not forget the Greeks and their quirky beliefs about odd and even numbers. They thought odd numbers were male and even numbers were female. Talk about taking gender reveal parties to a whole 'nother level. I can just imagine Socrates and Plato sitting around, arguing about whether nine is a macho stud or a sassy lady. Ah, the ancient philosophers and their weird priorities.

Then there's the 'Golden Ratio,' a number that has inspired artists and architects across centuries with its mesmerizing beauty. It's so perfect of a number that you just want to punch it in the face. However, the magical superstitious ones are cool, like how the number 'four' is considered unlucky in some East Asian cultures. At the same time, 'thirteen' is the black sheep in many Western societies. Ain't that something.

Anyway, enough rambling. Let's dive back into the silver-lined world of Kaspa. Brace yourself, my friend, because we're about to go down the rabbit hole of numbers. So many numbers.

The Numbers

The total supply of Kaspa is a mind-boggling 28.7 billion KAS. Yes, you heard me right, a billion with a capital 'B.' That's enough KAS to make Scrooge McDuck's vault look like pocket change. We're talking about a number so massive that if it was USD, it could fund a fleet of Smart cars or at least a lifetime supply of tacos. And I'm not talking about those sad, lukewarm tacos from the drive-thru. I'm talking about gourmet, mouth-watering, crunch-in-your-mouth tacos. Also, I should add the disclaimer here: I'm bad with numbers, especially regarding money.

This total supply number, yeah, it isn't going anywhere. It's as unchangeable as the laws of gravity or the fact that tacos are the most essential food group. Once it's set in the code, it's like the Ten Commandments carved in stone. No amount of begging, pleading, or sacrificing your Mike Zak action figure to the math gods will alter it.

In this grand symphony of monetary policy, Kaspa's emission schedule unfolds like a two-act play, each act as compelling as the other. As we venture into the first act, let us immerse ourselves in the grand theater of the mind. The Kaspa mainnet took its inaugural bow on that fateful day, November 7th, 2021. The stage was set, and the curtains were drawn back to reveal a world of possibilities. It was like the Big Bang of crypto round 2, the return of Satoshi, featuring Kaspa.

During the pre-deflationary phase, we experienced the wild ride of the random reward subphase. The reward rate danced before our eyes like a mischievous sprite, jumping randomly from 1 to 1000 KAS per block. The thrill of the unknown permeated the air, leaving us guessing with every twist and turn. Then, just as fast as it began, the 1st hard fork stormed onto the scene on May 8th, 2022, injecting a serum of stability into the network.

With the flick of a narrative switch, the reward rate found its equilibrium, settling gracefully at 500 KAS per second. A consistent and unwavering reward for participation in this exciting venture of risk. Each block, crafted with precision at a steady rate of one per second, bore the fruit of 500 KAS. It was a symphony of certainty amidst a sea of uncertainty, captivating us for a full six months.

The pre-deflationary phase of Kaspa's tokenomics was indeed an enthralling journey, akin to the initial chapters of a compelling novel. It left us craving more, eagerly turning the pages to see what lay ahead, and on cue, enter the second phase, the chromatic phase. This is where things start to get real. The block rewards now decrease geometrically, kicking off with an initial block reward of 440 KAS. This reward halved once yearly but smoothly, like the opposite of your last date.

In the chromatic phase, the block reward reduction wasn't a sudden drop; it was as smooth as a good transition between chapters. It happened gradually every month, each time by a factor of $(1/2)^{(1/12)}$. Now, if that confuses you, let's put it this way: it's just like the ratio of frequencies between two consecutive semitones in a tempered chromatic musical scale. Yep, Kaspa is just a jam band of mathematical harmonies.

A year is melodiously called an "octave," stretching across 365.25 days. And a month, ah, that's a "semitone," a sweet slice of time that spans precisely one-twelfth of a year. I double-checked the math, but you've already been warned.

Remember this important note: the policy dictates how many coins are minted per second, regardless of the block rate. The rewards are based on time, each second. Therefore, if the block rate changes in the future, the reward will be adjusted accordingly to maintain the same emission rate. It's like a conductor keeping the rhythm in check, ensuring the emission rate remains in perfect harmony.

And just like any musical score, our song has a tempo:

By January 1st, 2023, about 15.3 billion KAS had been mined, which accounts for 53.3% of the total supply. Fast forward to January 1st, 2024, and the KAS count will soar to around 21.9 billion, claiming a cool 76.3% of the total supply. And if you mark your calendars for January 1st, 2025, you'll witness the mining of approximately 25.1 billion KAS, making up 87.4% of the total supply. Finally, prepare for a suspenseful climax on July 10th, 2026, as about 95% of all KAS will have been mined, leaving us with just a few lingering coins left to be uncovered.

And when will the block reward go to zero, marking the end of our thrilling tale? Well, that will be roughly 36 years after the start of the mainnet.

Miners won't be left empty-handed after the emissions run their course and the final curtain falls. They'll still be rewarded for their hard work, but this time in the form of fees from transactions. Miners will reap the network they sow.

If these emission rates seem fast, it's because they are. When it comes to emission schedules, there's a lot to consider. Kaspa, with its lightning-fast pace, has a distinct advantage over its crypto counterparts. It's in a race against time, against other digital currencies, sprinting ahead with unrivaled enthusiasm and vigor. While some may argue that slow and steady wins the race, Kaspa refuses to conform to that old adage. It embraces the notion that speed can be a virtue, especially in digital currencies where competition is fierce.

But what makes a fast emission schedule so beneficial, you ask? Well, let me enlighten you, my curious comrades. First and foremost, it ensures a fair and widespread distribution of Kaspa coins. No one likes a snail's pace when it comes to divvying up the wealth. With a swift emission schedule, everyone can get their hands on some shiny Kaspa coins, spreading wealth and avoiding a monopolistic hoarder situation.

A fast emission schedule is like a consistent pulse of energy blasted wave after wave into the ecosystem. With an influx of new coins, users are encouraged to actively participate in transactions, mining, and trading. It's a bustling marketplace where everyone wants a piece of the action, creating a vibrant and dynamic environment that keeps us on our toes.

Kaspa's emission schedule is designed to wrap up within a lifetime. Yes, you heard that right. Our children and grandchildren won't have to deal with an unfinished network looming over their heads like a half-read book with missing pages.

Also, by the time those mighty ASICs (application-specific integrated circuits) come into play, which looks to be happening now, most of the emissions will have already been completed, which is currently around 65%. It's estimated that Kaspa will be about 70% mined when ASICs are fully rolled out. I don't get to say this much in life, but I love it when things go according to plan.

Ah, the ebb and flow of adoption rates and emission speeds: The Tale of Two Cryptos.

Not So Fast

Let's take a moment to appreciate Bitcoin, the granddaddy of them all, starting its journey like a cautious sea turtle testing the waters, aware that a seagull could swoop in for a feast at any moment. Naturally, the skeptics raised their eyebrows, unsure about this new-fangled digital currency. But as time passed, people began to grasp its potential, and the concept took hold.

Now, shift your gaze to Kaspa, the nimble newcomer in this fast-paced landscape. It blasted onto the scene on a Ducati Superleggera V4, leaving everyone in awe of its potential. It was the talk of the town, with folks lining up like it was a Black Friday sale. Kaspa had the innovation game on lock, and its enthusiastic community couldn't get enough. Popping a wheelie, leaving poor sea turtles sucking dust.

But here's the twist: despite Bitcoin's slow and steady emission pace, it was faster than Kaspa regarding emissions compared to adoption. It's a paradoxical observation that shows how speed is relative. Bitcoin's marathon-like emission rhythm proved that slow and steady can be fast. This little fringe case shows that Kaspa's emission speed is actually not fast, at least at first, when examining the factors beyond emission rates and weighing crypto adoption.

Also, when first launched, Kaspa decided to break the mold and defy expectations. In the spirit of Satoshi Nakamoto's philosophy, there was no initial coin offering (ICO) or token sale to secure funding for the network. Instead, Kaspa went for a fair launch, creating a level playing field for all. There was no premine, presale, or secret stash of coins waiting to be unleashed. Everyone had the same chance to earn KAS right from the start. It was a bold move, a conviction to equal opportunity and the power of decentralized finance.

Now, about the costs and fees that come with this grand narrative. The current transaction fee in the Kaspa ecosystem is 0.0001 KAS per

UTXO (unspent transaction output). Like super cheap. Insanely cheap. In digital currencies, transaction fees ensure the smooth functioning of the network and keep the wheels of progress turning. Miners need to earn, or miners don't work.

Now, let's delve into the complex world of max supply values. You might wonder why you see different max supply values in different places. Well, it's a bit like the ending of a well-written mystery novel—there's more than meets the eye. You see, the hard cap in the code is twenty-nine billion, but the actual supply is a bit elusive due to several factors.

Let's start with the "random reward subphase." It was like the unpredictable weather during the first two weeks of Kaspa's mainnet, where the block reward danced around like a capricious meteorological phenomenon. It ranged from 1 to 1000, making it difficult to predict whether you'll need an umbrella, a sunhat, or a parka. The expected average was 500, but in reality, it veered closer to 750, adding about an additional 300 million to the estimated supply of the "stable reward" phase. It's like the unexpected plot twist that keeps you on the edge of your seat or that cliffhanger that never gives closure.

Then there's the complexity of the halving schedule based on the Difficulty Adjustment Algorithm score (DAA) calculation. As the DAA score can vary slightly for each node in real-time, not all nodes have the same view of all blocks generated at any given moment. Each node makes an independent call on whether it's time for a reward reduction, causing minor variations in the total emission. It's like different chefs using the same recipe for cooking a dish but adding their own special ingredients, resulting in weird fusion food that's also confused about what it's supposed to be.

But despite all these fluctuations, the total emission is guaranteed never to reach twenty-nine billion. The most accurate estimate available, given by a trustworthy bot in Discord, is 28,704,026,601 KAS over a span of thirty-six years from the mainnet start. It's a complex formula, but it keeps things fair, transparent, and adds just the right amount of unpredictability.

Back in the wild and untamed realm of computer mining, Kaspa embarked on its journey with CPUs (Central Processing Unit), but it wasn't long before the powerful GPUs (Graphics processing unit) erupted onto the scene. It was like going from riding a horse to piloting a jet, an exciting era of rapid advancement and adaptation. These GPUs didn't just settle for mediocrity. They embraced dual mining and made their mark on the Kaspa landscape, leaving a trail of innovation in their wake.

Along came the FPGAs (Field-programmable gate array), setting up shop alongside the GPUs like neighboring towns sharing resources. It was a time of even more significant technological leaps, where ingenuity and efficiency held hands and danced a lively jig. They changed the game, just like the dawn of agriculture in the age of nomads, transforming everything in their path and promising unparalleled productivity and effectiveness. They were the trailblazers, doing to GPUs what GPUs did to CPUs, catapulting the network to new heights of technological prowess.

And now, the era of ASICs has arrived, heralding both excitement and uncertainty. These ASICs are the hot topic, the latest gadget everyone wants to get their hands on. They promise unparalleled efficiency, like having a turbocharged engine under the hood, and just as loud. But what sets them apart is their unwavering dedication to the cause. No matter the circumstances, they'll keep on mining, raising the network hash rate and standing as a stalwart defense against 51% of attacks.

They're like the loyal soldiers guarding the integrity of the network, and that's something to admire.

But let's not forget our trusty GPUs. They mined a significant chunk of the KAS supply during their reign. They were like the gold miners of the digital world, extracting their treasures and selling them to cover their mining costs. It was a way to distribute the wealth, like miners selling their gold to different buyers. However, these GPUs were fair-weather friends. They could switch their allegiances to other coins if they promised greener pastures. Loyalty can be fickle.

On the other hand, ASICs are a different breed. They're designed specifically for mining Kaspa's kHeavyHash, and that's where their heart lies. No matter what's happening in the crypto world, they'll keep mining for Kaspa. They're like the true-blue companions who stick with you through thick and thin. Their unwavering commitment raises the network hash rate and fortifies it against potential attacks, serving as a dependable army guarding the fortress.

The Mining Shift
Regarding the future of Kaspa mining, GPUs may have had their fun in the sun. Nonetheless, they'll

still coexist with ASICs for a while longer before ASICs genuinely take over the scene. However, keep your eyes on the horizon because the era of oPoW photonic ASICs may be coming. They're the champions of heightened security and low energy consumption, a dream come true for efficiency. With these new ASICs, the shift in mining costs will be significant, leaning more toward capital expenses and reducing operational costs. A true revolution in the mining landscape.

In the epic tale of Kaspa, we find ourselves standing at the crossroads of mining and tokenomics. These two pillars shape the very essence of this remarkable blockchain. Together, they orchestrate a symphony of supply, demand, and technological evolution, harmonizing to create a landscape of fairness, accessibility, and endless possibilities.

Like a virtuoso musician, mining plays a crucial role in this grand composition. Armed with powerful hardware and unwavering determination, miners dedicate their computing power to secure the network, validate transactions, and bring new KAS coins into existence. They are the ones who extract digital gold from the depths of the blockchain's code and secure the network mineshaft with their resources.

But mining is not merely about extracting coins; it is an integral part of the greater tokenomic narrative. It ensures the fair and widespread distribution of KAS, preventing monopolistic hoarding and fostering a vibrant ecosystem where participants from all walks of life have a chance to partake in digital wealth.

Tokenomics, on the other hand, acts as the conductor of this symphony, guiding the rhythm and flow of the KAS supply. It defines the emission schedule, carefully balancing the rate at which new coins are minted with the network's demand and adoption. Through meticulous calculations and adjustments, tokenomics maintains a delicate equilibrium, ensuring a sustainable and thriving ecosystem.

As we turn our gaze toward the future, where mining and tokenomics continue their harmonious dance, with each block mined, the network grows more substantial, and the distribution of KAS becomes more widespread. The symphony of tokenomics ensures that everyone can participate, transact, and stake their claim in the digital frontier.

Chapter 7

Regarding the Rust Rewrite

As you walk down the quiet digital corridors of the Kaspa network, where the binary footfalls echo with a profound sense of urgency, there's a deep air of expectancy. From the hard-coded recesses of the Kaspa Discord server to the viral Tweets that parrot the farthest corners of the globe. Something is different; something extraordinary is afoot. The anticipation is a tangible presence, electrifying the air, making the pixels on the screen dance with barely contained excitement. Could it be a new season of the Kardashians? A blockchain monkey pic? Dubstep?

The soft whispers build into a collective roar echoing through the crypto sphere. The chant, gaining momentum, is heard far and wide across the digital landscape. Rust! Rust! Rust! It's the battle cry of a community ready to embrace change. It's the rallying call of an army eager for a brighter, swifter, more adaptable future. It's the name that holds the promise to propel our dear Kaspa network into a realm of undiscovered potential.

And as you cheer on, eagerly joining the intoxicating call-to-action, you're probably asking yourself, "What even is Rust, and why am I chanting in Starbucks?"

While I can't explain your mad ramblings in Starbucks, I can tell you that Rust is a programming language, and not just any language. It's a language that sets the hearts of coders ablaze. Renowned for its kickass performance and its unflinching reliability, Rust is the VIP pass that grants us entrance into a future of faster processing speeds and bulletproof stability.

Since it was first announced as a Kaspa Improvement Proposal (KIP) to rewrite Kaspa in Rust, the idea has taken on a life of its own. What started as a humble beginning of developers brainstorming in the shadows of Discord has now transformed into a tangible reality, a real-world project on the verge of shifting gears from the Alpha preflight checklist to the exciting test flight of Beta.

This redesign from Go to Rust isn't just a code rewrite. It's a transformation, a metamorphosis of sorts. Picture our Kaspa network, a hardworking 1998 Honda Accord, carting us around dutifully from place to place, then we slap a giant rocket booster on its back. The same car with the same reliability but much faster. Blasting through tasks, flying over obstacles, its codebase gleaming in the sunlight of efficiency, ready to take on the world with renewed vigor.

Much like my bank account, codebases tend to accumulate a heap of technical debt over the years. Bits and bobs of dusty Go-based structures scattered about, cobwebs in every corner. But with the Rust rewrite on the horizon, it's like Kaspa's about to get the mother of all spring cleans. This grand makeover is set to clear the path for fresh upgrades; like the room to grow some spiffy smart contract support and a sleek new consensus ordering algorithm. Who doesn't love that new protocol smell?

And let's not ignore the pièce de résistance of Rusty Kaspa: Performance. Yes, ladies and gents, you heard right. Thanks to Rust's stellar high-level constructs, the system will churn out blocks and transactions like a finely-tuned machine. Leaving the old processing speeds choking on its dust. Faster, tougher, superior—that's the future for Kaspa. And that translates to a slicker, more seamless user experience for you, me, and the rest of the world.

A full node written in Rust was implemented in the beginning phase, incorporating all core logic and algorithms. This approach aimed to maintain crucial functionalities while adding the performance edge of Rustlang. The expected result was a hybrid node offering a transitory blend of stability, speed, and flexibility.

The ambitions were as vast as the night sky, with performance improvement being the North Star guiding our journey. We dreamed of ramping up single-core performance and capitalizing on the power of multi-core scaling. With its no-nonsense attitude toward garbage collection, Rust was the secret sauce, the ace in the hole. When paired with nifty database optimizations, the promise of substantial runtime enhancements shimmered on the horizon, like constructing a well-engineered city where every building, road, and utility had a distinct purpose, yet together they formed a model of urban efficiency. That's the beauty of independent task parallelism—it allowed consensus block and transaction processing to mesh like the intricate gears of a Swiss watch, optimizing and heightening the system's overall performance.

But that's not where Rusty Kaspa stopped showing off its potential. On the network level, it was like the magician Elichai, pulling an endless string of colorful handkerchiefs from his Kaspa-branded trucker hat. New features, such as archival nodes on a peer-to-peer (P2P) basis and header compression at the P2P level, began to surface. These enhancements were our answer to streamlining operations and turbocharging overall network performance.

TPS & BPS

When it comes to crypto people, they usually get all gooey-eyed over transactions per second or TPS. However, in the Kaspa cosmos, the star of the show is the estimated 32 blocks per second (BPS). Why, you ask? Well, it's all thanks to its fancy blockDAG.

In the Kaspa world, blocks don't politely wait their turn to get added one after another. They party together. They're added all at once. This means this system can handle more transactions and get confirmations done faster. Why? Simply because they've thrown the usual stand-in-line-for-your-turn model out of the window. Transactions here don't have to twiddle their thumbs, waiting for a line of blocks to get confirmed.

So, with this kind of setup, Kaspa is dreaming big. We're talking sky-high, stratosphere big. They're aiming for a heart-stopping, you-gotta-be-kidding-me 100 BPS!

But the only way to discover if this pipe dream can be a reality is by running the good old fashion tests. The Kaspa crew knows what they're doing, and what they do is always expert-level. It's a delicate juggling between pumping up the block mining and keeping the header size in proportion.

The Rust Ripple

The Rust rewrite isn't just about blasting off toward a 100 BPS on the mainnet, either. No, it's a slow and calculated adventure excavation the likes of Indiana Jones. Unearthing untapped efficiencies, spelunking the uncharted cyber civilizations and digital mysteries that this rewrite would lay before us. Equipped with Rustlang as its weapon, Kaspa was on the cusp of a new era, primed to make intelligent, calculated decisions to carve its future path.

When the news broke on Twitter that the Rustlang implementation was operating seamlessly on the mainnet, hinting that the first stable version of Rusty Kaspa might be just around the corner, the development signaled the possibility of accelerating block rates on the test net, reinforcing Kaspa's standing as the fastest proof-of-work blockchain.

Michael Sutton, one of the key figures spearheading Rusty Kaspa, showcased a screenshot of an experimental Rust node syncing live on the mainnet. This was no ordinary step; it was a significant stride, a resounding affirmation of the developer's countless hours and Herculean efforts to push the boundaries of what Kaspa could achieve. It's fair to say that a few additional cold ones probably met their demise in celebration of this monumental achievement.

Upgrades

As Kaspa plunged headfirst into its initial cycle of stability enhancements, a few critical areas were on its radar, such as refining the P2P connection management. P2P is the technology that allows Kaspa nodes to connect and communicate directly with each other rather than through a centralized server. It's the backbone of a decentralized network like Kaspa, and optimizing it means a more robust and efficient network overall.

The Remote Procedure Call (RPC) APIs were put under the microscope. RPCs allow network components to communicate and perform operations, essentially letting a program call a function on another computer as if on the same machine. By refining the RPC APIs, Kaspa aimed to make these calls smoother and more effective.

The devs also focused on the Command Line Interface (CLI) APIs. A CLI is a text-based interface that interacts with software and operating systems. Kaspa planned to provide users with more flexible, efficient, and powerful ways to interact with the network by improving the CLI APIs.

Rusty Kaspa didn't overlook the importance of addressing critical algorithmic edge cases. While these instances are not everyday occurrences, they are fundamental in maintaining the system's security. Ignoring them could lead to extreme vulnerabilities. For example, you wouldn't construct a building without considering a stable foundation first, right? Leaning Tower of Pisa?

It's the dawn of April 15th, 2023; El Chapo is in the news again; well, his sons are now, I guess, and the air is thick with the collective excitement of the Kaspa community. There's a palpable buzz of suspense, a fervor that comes with a significant shift in the landscape, once again, all the folks waiting with bated breath. They're finally about to have a front-row seat to the debut of the Alpha version of 'Rusty Kaspa'—not just a great album release but a meaningful step in the evolution of the network.

The Kaspa network has both a test net and mainnet functioning as two different playgrounds, and Alpha binaries of each were released. The Alpha testnet is like the rehearsal stage where all the bugs and glitches are worked out; it's the environment where the Rusty Kaspa can stretch its legs, run wild, and be subjected to severe stress tests, cranking the BPS to surreal levels. If the Testnet stumbled a bit, there are no real-world consequences, so it's used and abused. In contrast, the mainnet is the main event, the big show—it's the real-world network where everything has to run smoothly and efficiently. Alpha mainnet runs Rust nodes in tandem with Go nodes to create a temporary mixed network. However, mining on the mainnet is restricted until Beta.

Now, when we talk about 'binaries,' we're not delving into the world of 'ones and zeros,' well, not exactly. In this context, binaries are the ready-to-run versions of a program. These compact, high-performance packages have been tailored to fit specific platforms, all set to be deployed.

The grand plan for this Alpha release isn't just a cosmetic touch-up. Oh no, it's poised to thoroughly renovate the Kaspa network; designed to elevate its level of decentralization, amplify performance, bolster security, and scale it up to maximum speeds.

Despite being in its Alpha stage, Rusty Kaspa was already making waves. The software had been running on both the mainnet and testnet, exhibited optimal performance, and was clear of any significant issues. However, the process of reaching the Beta release would put astronaut camp to shame with Alpha's rigorous testing and refinement.

The roadmap to the Beta release was laced with several crucial tasks. First, the infrastructure had to be primed to handle increased block rates. This called for automating the pruning of block headers and block sampling for difficulty adjustment. Then, the system needed to be equipped with the ability to recover from interrupted Initial Block Downloads (IBD) and an enhanced API.

Addressing the automatic pruning of block headers was a significant accomplishment as well. In the existing scenario, clearing older header data demanded a manual node resync. With Rust, this process became more streamlined and efficient, reducing overhead and boosting performance.

Also, a new Rust-based transaction generation tool by the-artist-formerly-known-as-Ori Newman, was designed for the test net. This tool aimed to maintain stable high Transactions Per Second (TPS) on the test net, enabling all components to cope with the increased load effectively.

Addressing the hard fork required to increase BPS was still on. Altering several consensus constants at the hard fork point was tricky. The developers were contemplating the launch of a new testnet as an alternative. Still, the decision was yet to be finalized, and the hard fork schedule was due to be published.

As April turned into May, the focus was all about "on-the-fly Header Pruning," a feature introduced by developer Michael Sutton. This innovative functionality allowed the automatic deletion of outdated or excessive data, comparable to a self-sufficient gardener constantly trimming back any dead branches to maintain the vitality of a tree. In the digital world of the Kaspa network, this pruning process worked tirelessly and automatically to eliminate redundant or outdated data, keeping the network streamlined, efficient, and healthy.

The 'on-the-fly' characteristic was crucial. Unlike the manual intervention and regular maintenance needed in the older pruning systems, this new feature did its job continuously and without disruption, allowing the Kaspa network to remain trimmed, compact, and uninterrupted. It also reduced the hard drive space requirements to around 4–6GB under current mainnet settings and transaction throughput. Finally, a diet that works and works fast.

But why is this so important? In the context of the Kaspa network, the faster the BPS, the quicker transactions can be processed and confirmed. Pruning plays a vital role here, ensuring that this increase in speed doesn't compromise efficiency. Likewise, removing redundant data allows the system to operate more smoothly and handle transactions more rapidly. This is probably why my smartphone's performance crawls; it's not like I can just get rid of my 4k Lego Movie collection.

This technical upgrade lowered the hardware barriers for running a node on the Kaspa network. Thanks to the smaller database size and quicker network syncs, running a node no longer necessitated high-end or expensive hardware. This was instrumental in preserving the network's decentralization, a fundamental principle of blockchain technology.

Nevertheless, incorporating this upgrade wasn't a walk in the park. The developers had to ensure that the network's 'connectivity'—the ability of one data block to communicate with another—wasn't disrupted while pruning unnecessary data. The solution to this complex problem was found in an elegant methodology presented in a 1989 research paper, "Efficient management of transitive relationships in large data and knowledge bases." Yeah, I got stuck on the title, too. I didn't even try to read further.

This algorithm allowed the pruning process and the routine acceptance of new data blocks to occur simultaneously, thereby eliminating potential delays. This meant Kaspa network users wouldn't experience any 'pauses' or slowdowns while the system conducted its data-clearing operations.

A Rusty Foundation for the Future
As Rusty Kaspa continues to evolve, it's opening up a wealth of new opportunities for both developers and users. The switch to Rust is about much more than simply improving the codebase; it's also about expanding Kaspa's functionality, positioning it as

the perfect foundation for innovative projects like the world's first parameterless protocol, DAG KNIGHT.

The Rust language is renowned for its speed, reliability, and ability to create highly concurrent systems, making it an ideal choice for high-performance applications like Kaspa. By moving to Rust, the Kaspa devs are setting the stage to develop exciting new features and possibilities, including Layer 2 solutions and smart contracts.

Layer 2 solutions are designed to improve a blockchain's scalability, efficiency, and speed. By handling transactions off-chain and only settling the net results on-chain, Layer 2 solutions can significantly reduce transaction costs and increase speed, making it possible to process thousands of transactions per second.

Smart contracts are another significant development in the pipeline. By enabling programmable transactions that automatically execute when certain conditions are met, smart contracts can create a wide range of decentralized applications (dApps), from DeFi protocols to decentralized exchanges and much more.

Kaspa's move to Rustlang also provides developers with a safer and more robust programming environment. Rust's focus on safety, particularly concerning memory safety, concurrency, and system-level programming, reduces the likelihood of bugs and security vulnerabilities, thereby reducing the risk and cost associated with building on the Kaspa platform. This robustness, safety, and Rustlang's performance characteristics make it an ideal platform for developers to build cutting-edge applications.

One such application that stands to benefit significantly from the Rust rewrite is DAG KNIGHT. Designed to leverage the benefits of the blockDAG architecture, DAG KNIGHT is set to take full advantage of Rusty Kaspa's robustness, efficiency, and flexibility. The Rust-based Kaspa will provide DAG KNIGHT with a solid, reliable foundation, allowing it to focus on delivering its unique value proposition without worrying about the underlying infrastructure.

By providing a more stable, scalable, and efficient codebase, the Rust rewrite enhances the Kaspa network and creates a more conducive environment for developers and users alike. It lays the groundwork for a new generation of dApps, paving the way for increased adoption and opening up exciting new possibilities for the Kaspa community.

Rusty Kaspa will become a game-changer in the crypto space as it continues to evolve and improve. With its focus on performance, safety, and scalability, it is poised to drive Kaspa's growth and innovation, creating a more vibrant and dynamic ecosystem for developers and users alike. Not to mention crushing BPS world records for any crypto network, ever.

The completion of Rusty Kaspa marks the beginning of a new era for Kaspa. It's not just about the technical improvements; it's about the new opportunities and possibilities it opens up. It's about creating a platform that developers can build on with confidence and that users can rely on for their needs. It's about building a future where the potential of the blockDAG architecture can be fully realized. It's about taking Kaspa to the next level.

Chapter 8

Kaspa in Practice, Present, and Future

Envision a world where cryptocurrencies aren't just status symbols, where they lounge off-chain as wasted data in a wallet for nothing more than bragging rights. Instead, they're spent. Not just burned, swapped, or traded. In this world, crypto is actually being used for commerce, and every moment quickens the pulse of the global economic heartbeat. That's what Kaspa is. Kaspa is meant to be the future of everyday transactions, and luckily, that future is now.

Cryptocurrency, even Kaspa, can often feel like trying to decrypt an alien language while being pelted with paintballs. It's all a bit much to take in, and just when you feel like you have a good grasp, *Bam!* Shot down by cryptography once again. But Kaspa is delightfully simple, a breath of fresh air when it comes to its use and mission. It's a digital diplomat, mediating between the cryptic realm of digital assets and everyday reality. It's promising us a world where secure, scalable, and efficient transactions are not just a pipe dream but the norm.

Kaspa is bound and determined, on a journey into the practical terrain of real-world applications. Whether it's for groceries, bills, tickets, that poor excuse for a drying rack, or the exercise bike you have only ever used like twice, this sprightly cryptocurrency can inject itself into our quotidian lives with the ease of a practiced social butterfly, offering an alternative to traditional financial systems as palatable as Rhubarbarian's homegrown maple syrup.

Kaspa vs TradFi

Let's think of the internet as a sprawling digital ecumenopolis—a breathtaking construct of human curiosity. It's a realm that's perpetually buzzing, continuously evolving, and never hitting the pause button. Yet, within this vast cyberspace network, a quiet and mighty force is at work: microtransactions. They're the diminutive, diligent champions of the digital business world, scattered like industrious ants, upholding economies, establishing intricate infrastructures, and enabling the smooth flow of digital goods and services.

However, as it often goes in stories worth telling, we encounter a formidable antagonist. In this scenario, traditional payment systems play the villain—throwing a wrench in the works of our microtransaction scene with their excessive processing fees. These greedy systems drain the potential of everyday trade like an aardvark slurping down our transaction ants. Admittedly, it's not the most pleasant of visuals, but villains seldom paint a pretty picture.

Emerging from these challenges, Kaspa strides forward, exuding the confidence of a seasoned professional and the unflinching resolve of a mountaineer set on conquering Everest. While it doesn't offer gimmicky extras like a catchy theme song or a secret hideout, Kaspa does bring a potent tool to the field: a blockDAG-powered infrastructure. This pioneering technical framework empowers it to handle a deluge of transactions simultaneously, all while meticulously slashing transaction costs to their bare minimum.

This advantage proves to be a game-changer for digital commerce. Consider e-commerce platforms that deal with countless microtransactions daily. Thanks to Kaspa's streamlined transaction process and reduced costs, these platforms can significantly increase efficiency and offer more competitive prices to customers. Moreover, with instant payment settlements, e-commerce platforms can drastically improve cash flow, an essential factor for businesses operating on thin margins.

Businesses that depend on global supply chains stand to benefit tremendously. By employing Kaspa, they can execute cross-border transactions without incurring exorbitant fees or dealing with extended wait times, bringing a new level of fluidity to international commerce.

Let's remember the smaller digital entrepreneurs, who can now viably sell low-cost items or services online, something previously untenable due to high fees. This ability opens up a whole new world of microeconomics, fostering a digital marketplace that's as diverse as it is vibrant.

Here's where we voyage from the ethereal corridors of the digital world to the tangible, touch-and-feel marketplace of retail. We've established that Kaspa is a blinding star in the digital cosmos, but it doesn't plan to stay in the void. On the contrary, it's also ready to prove its worthiness in our brick-and-mortar transactions. As the waves of cryptocurrencies wash over our societal shores, we're all secretly (or not-so-secretly) itching to swap out those grimy old bills, useless coins, and annoying chip cards that never work for an effortless digital currency.

Sporting the scalability of an infinite spreadsheet and bearing transaction fees so slender a blade of grass looks portly, Kaspa and businesses together form a sweet chorus, a song of tantalizing potential, reduced costs, and streamlined efficiency. It's an attractive prospect, whether you're operating a delightful hole-in-the-wall music shop or making calls as a worldwide retail juggernaut.

Kaspa steps in with an irresistible proposition, taking a sledgehammer to the infuriating transaction fees in which traditional payment systems seem to feast upon businesses. Plus, it offers a protective shield against the dreaded chargeback monster, a ghoul that plagues the slumber of many a retailer. No money is no problem because it just means there is no money. You actually cannot spend what you don't have.

For everyday consumers, transactions become as smooth as Wolfie's voice on a Saturday night AMA, privacy gets a robust upgrade, and the tantalizing prospect of saving money becomes a reality. It's as though Kaspa is serving as a gilded bridge, connecting the somewhat mysterious world of cryptocurrencies to the practical realm of day-to-day transactions.

Trustless

Considering the cornerstone of blockchain technology, one feature really gets the enthusiasts' pulse racing: peer-to-peer payments—the magic of conjuring up a digital coin and sending it directly from your virtual wallet to another person's, bypassing traditional banking systems, leaving the astonished faces of traditional bankers in frustrated silence, unable to charge their customary commission. En garde middleman-man!

These are the fabled 'trustless' transactions. Now, 'trustless' may sound like a negative term, but it's quite the opposite in the context of crypto. It essentially means you don't have to trust the person you're transacting with or any third-party intermediary, for that matter. Instead, Kaspa's robust infrastructure ensures that each transaction is independently verifiable and irreversible, providing a level of security comparable to that of a fortified bank.

In essence, Kaspa enhances the experience of peer-to-peer transactions by making them quicker, safer, and more economical. It's not just the change in our pockets that Kaspa is after but a difference in how we handle and perceive daily transactions, making the integration of cryptocurrency into our everyday lives more seamless and practical.

The Future of Commerce

So, now it's a warm Friday evening. You're out with a delightful mix of friends, colleagues, and the odd neighbor, hauntedcook. You've all convened at your favorite spot, a place that serves the kind of food that makes your taste buds sing with joy. Think of a gastronomic congregation of succulent burgers, perfectly crispy fries, and decadent desserts, all washed down with a locally brewed craft beer. The atmosphere is buzzing, laughter is in the air, and the food is divine. It's shaping up to be a great evening.

However, like a dark cloud on the horizon, the end of the meal approaches. And with it, the arrival of the bill. The jovial chatter around the table drops a notch, and the daunting prospect of dividing the cost among everyone looms large. You're left wondering if you should have paid more attention in math class instead of writing terrible punk-rock lyrics in a notebook. However, let's get back to the present in the future. You're equipped with your smartphone's secret weapon, the Kaspium mobile wallet.

With a scan of the QR code on the bill, a barely audible beep, Ormass' avatar flashes on the screen, and just like that, the bill is paid. No more hasty calculations, no more awkward reminders to friends about their share, and most importantly, no more waiting for everyone to dig out their credit cards or checkbooks. With the Kaspium mobile wallet, the process of payments has been turned on its head, catapulting us straight into the future of finance.

Let's expand this everyday scenario to something more significant—international transfers. For many, this process is as integral to their lives as a hearty breakfast but often equally as frustrating. The current money transfer system feels like biking while wearing a blindfold. It's cumbersome, complicated, and riddled with potholes.

Innumerable fees seem to multiply like gremlins every time you look away, and the processing times can feel akin to the pace of a tired sloth on a lazy afternoon. Such hassles could lead even the most patient person to a moment of sheer frustration, compelling them to rethink their life choices. *If only the punk-rock band stayed together…*

Kaspa, as a seasoned athlete, is agile and swift, navigating through the maze of international transactions. It leaps over the borders with ease, whizzing past the obstacles of varying currencies and regional regulations. In. An. Instant. You can send money anywhere in the world in a flash.

Intermediaries often seem to loom like vultures, waiting to take a chunk out of your hard-earned money. With the introduction of Kaspa, these intermediaries are given a swift kick into oblivion. The suited executives who once treated your money like their cash piñata are no longer part of the equation. It's just you and your Kaspa wallet. This new-age digital wallet ensures you retain more of your income, a crucial aspect in a world where every penny can make a difference.

Steering a business, no matter its size is a lot like performing acrobatics, on a pirate ship, during a storm, with a crew that's just discovered the rum is all gone. There's a sense of controlled chaos, a hint of imminent disaster, and a dash of desperation. The constant pressure to keep everything running smoothly, efficiently, and profitably is a feat akin to juggling flaming torches. So, when a tool like Kaspa strides onto the scene, it's as welcome as an ice-cold beer at the end of a long day of moderating on a red market day.

Low transaction costs that would make even the thriftiest of accountants cry. Transaction times so swift a jet fighter would blackout. No more agonizing waits for the cogs of traditional banking to sluggishly turn and clear transactions. No more wasting precious time that could be better spent concocting plans for world domination (or at least market domination). Whether transferring funds to an overseas supplier or rewarding your diligent employees, Kaspa has your back.

It's as if the software developers and designers behind Kaspa took a long, hard look at the pain points of running a business and decided to build a financial miracle machine. The versatility and convenience of this platform make it a powerful ally in any business arsenal.

But that's not all. Kaspa brings along its trusty sidekick—the blockDAG. With this technology, businesses can enhance transparency to a degree that was previously unthinkable. Transactions are recorded and traceable, offering a level of accountability that's like having an auditor perched on your shoulder 24/7. This one doesn't need perfect paperwork, sick leaves, or yearly bonuses.

This level of traceability would make a true crime show envious as you zoom in on every detail of a financial transaction. It means improved quality control, better risk management, and a comprehensive view of how money moves within your organization. It's like having a financial magnifying glass that highlights what's working, what's not, and where there's room for improvement.

Whether at the helm of a multinational corporation with a supply chain stretching across continents or the proud proprietor of a quaint little bakery in a quaint town, Kaspa comes in handy. Helping you keep all your transactions orderly, from the purchase of raw materials to the payment of staff salaries.

Kaspa does more than just make transactions easier. It transforms how you operate your business, allowing you to focus on the big picture—be it expanding your empire, perfecting your grandma's secret muffin recipe, or maybe just figuring out how to keep the rum supply on your imaginary pirate ship well-stocked. Because in the world of business, every helping hand (or advanced digital payment platform) counts.

The Further in the Future of Commerce
Soon, there will be a world where your gadgets hold entire conversations with each other while you sleep. A world where your devices don't just silently work for you but actively hustle, transact, and make decisions on your behalf. No, I'm not describing some futuristic sci-fi tech. Wait... or am I? Anyway, I'm talking about the here and now with the Internet of Things (IoT).

The IoT is the global gabfest of devices, where your smartphone, your fridge, your car, and your robot... (we don't judge) all join in on a virtual chinwag across the web. It's like a never-ending high school reunion with less drama and more fun. But there's a catch. For these gadgets to really tap-dance to their full potential, they need a way to exchange digital currency. And who better to serve as the trustworthy middleman in this high-tech tango than our trusty compadre, Kaspa?

Before you say, "Hang on a second, no way is my vacuum spending my hard-earned KAS," let me delve into some examples. Suppose you're comfortably nestled on your couch halfway through a nail-biting thriller, and the last thing you want to do is disrupt your cinematic immersion to refuel your car for tomorrow's commute. Wouldn't it be nice if your car, in its quiet automotive wisdom, could head to the gas station, refuel itself, and settle the bill, all while you remain transfixed by the plot twists of *The Wire* unfolding on your screen?

Or consider your smart fridge a devoted sentinel guarding your dairy supplies. You're low on milk—a critical component of your morning coffee ritual. Rather than flashing annoying warning lights or pushing alerts to your already cluttered smartphone, it simply orders a fresh supply, pays for it, and arranges for it to be dropped at your doorstep, all in time for your breakfast.

This is the potential of a world empowered by Kaspa and IoT. Picture it as an intricate network of connected gadgets, each device fulfilling its specific role, all seamlessly coordinated under the able guidance of Kaspa.

Think of it as the grease in the IoT machine, helping things move smoothly and efficiently. It enables an ecosystem where devices are not just connected for communication but also for commerce. Kaspa's ability to swiftly handle high volumes of transactions, no matter how minute, allows the IoT to truly stretch its legs and sprint toward a future that promises even more convenience, efficiency, and automation. Personally, I can't wait for my smart toaster to negotiate a deal on a premium loaf of potato bread. Technology is wild.

The Evolution

So, we've jaunted through the kaleidoscopic landscape of Kaspa's potential applications. We've seen how this trailblazing cryptocurrency could slip into our daily lives with the grace and smoothness of a well-rehearsed Broadway number. Yet, let's not mistake Kaspa as some brand of flashy digital wizardry, destined to be trapped within the confounding realms of tech geeks and financial gurus. Far from it.

Kaspa is about elevating our mundane routines, about injecting a dollop of convenience into our busy lives. A dedicated backstage hand tirelessly working to ensure the show goes on without a hitch. It's about transforming our perception of financial transactions from something as exciting as watching paint dry to potentially having the appeal of a captivating page-turner.

Even as we marvel at its current abilities, Kaspa continues to evolve, grow, and adapt. It's nudging at the boundaries of our understanding of what a cryptocurrency can, and perhaps should, be. Kaspa seems set to redefine our expectations and experience of financial transactions, promising to turn the ordinary into the extraordinary.

Chapter 9

Charting a Course

Humanity. One moment you're youthful and agile, swiftly maneuvering through life with the world at your fingertips. The next, you find yourself squinting over bifocals, struggling to read small print and emitting suspicious groans whenever you rise from your well-used recliner. But that's the essence of the human adventure, isn't it? We're all enrolled in the aging academy, where our individual biology determines our curriculum, graded by our exercise routines and fast-food diets.

Yet, as we progress from agile to achy, something extraordinary occurs in the realm of our creations: technology. This intrepid offspring of the human intellect seems to exist in a parallel reality where each passing year doesn't bring a slowdown but an acceleration, a runaway speed-up.

In our younger, impatient days, technology mirrored our pace. It consisted of large computers, slow modems, and pixelated screens. But as we aged and slowed down, technology, with a mischievous glimmer in its digital eyes, chose a different path. It became like a rebellious teenager who once imitated us but now surpasses us, growing, advancing, and evolving at a speed that defies time itself.

While Moore's Law predicts technological growth, it serves as a rhythmic backbone in the symphony of progress, driving but not defining the music. True magic emerges when innovative minds take this underlying tempo and overlay it with their own visionary melodies. We've witnessed this symphony evolve, and now, as the music swells, we approach a crescendo where the harmonies of technology, cryptography, and society converge to create an intricate and captivating jazz performance.

This is where the rhythm of innovation converges with the cool contemporary jazz fusion of cryptography and social dynamics. They dance together in harmony, like a skilled drummer playing a swing beat. The spotlight shifts, illuminating the digital stage where disruptive innovation takes center stage.

Making his entrance is a fresh talent, a maestro shaped by the artful skills of a techno-craftsman known by the pseudonym azbuky. This virtuoso has orchestrated a performance where every movement and every note resounds with the essence of progress. Prepare to be captivated by his masterpiece: Kaspium, the Kaspa mobile wallet. It's a culmination of digital mastery that strikes all the right chords in the symphony of financial excellence. Party on, Garth!

Now, what is it about Kaspium that generates anticipation in the binary jazz club? Finding yourself in the club's heart, immersed in its urban symphony. Suddenly, you feel the urge to make a purchase. Perhaps it's the cover of Billy Cobham's Red Baron, but you just need to get your hands on a biplane. Or, more likely, support an ambitious indie flying sim game on Kickstarter, even though it may never see completion. Star Citizen, I'm looking at you.

In the past, you would have rushed home, booted up your sluggish PC, and navigated through a cumbersome sea of browser tabs to complete the transaction. But those days are as outdated as smoke signals. Welcome to the era of Kaspium. With a simple flick of your smartphone, Kaspium becomes your personal bank, allowing you to conduct transactions as effortlessly as waving a wand. It's a seamless evolution of convenience, with less abracadabra and more streamlined efficiency.

Kaspium serves as a rock-solid vault, a fortress safeguarding your valuable digital assets. This cyber stronghold boasts a user-friendly interface akin to your favorite social media app yet equipped with the impenetrability of Fort Knox. With intuitive ease, Kaspium guarantees a transactional experience smoother than John Travolta on the dance floor. Additionally, it supports smartphone biometrics, providing an extra layer of security and convenience.

One notable feature of Kaspium is its QR code transaction functionality. No longer will you grapple with lengthy digital addresses resembling CVS receipts. With Kaspium, it's as simple as scanning a QR code, a personal access code to the digital world. It's a straightforward point-and-scan operation devoid of any Hackerman complexity.

Kaspium is no half-baked idea concocted in azbuky's garage. On the contrary, this digital wallet is live in Beta, rigorously tested, evaluated, and refined to perfection on iOS and Android platforms. Every cog and feature is meticulously examined and polished, just like preparing a race car for the Indy

500. After all, you wouldn't hit the track with only three tires.

In the Kaspa ecosystem, progress is not dictated by the ticking of a clock but by the quality of each tick and the value added with each tock. Rather than marking calendars or setting countdown timers, we can sit back and await the unfolding magic. When Kaspium strides onto the world stage, it will not be a mere event but a revelation, a significant shift in the Kaspa paradigm, empowering you with the might of KAS in the palm of your hand.

Developments

In a world where change is the only constant, each variation presents new challenges, each setback an enigma waiting to be deciphered. As we prepared to unite Kaspa, our vibrant crypto-protocol, with Ledger, it felt like orchestrating a social gathering with guests spanning different time zones. We were exuberant party planners eager to make every move count.

Ledger, a formidable fortress of security, stands as a haven for your digital treasures, shielding them from the perils of the online realm. Similar to a personal Swiss bank vault, Ledger offers a secure sanctuary where your investments remain insulated from the malevolent intentions of online scammers. This hardware wallet allows you to store cryptographic keys offline, safeguarding your assets from the threats of the internet. It becomes your personal treasure trove, albeit filled with cryptocurrencies like Bitcoin, Ethereum, and the venerable Kaspa.

The integration of Kaspa with Ledger unfolded like a saga deserving of its trilogy. It commenced with ambitious fervor, a community eager to invest its faith and resources. However, just as in an M. Night Shyamalan film, the original developer, our code white knight, was struck by an unpredictable twist of fate, unable to reach the final act. In the blink of an eye, the community found itself caught in a suspenseful thriller, searching for the next move to keep the narrative alive.

Enter coderofstuff, our valiant digital squire armed with coding expertise. Did he possess an intricate understanding of the cryptographic conundrum at his fingertips? Eh, close enough. But he carried with him a compass of determination, armed with a roadmap sketched in ideas as ethereal as morning fog. Without missing a beat, he stepped into the dynamic narrative, assumed his role, and embarked on a quest to forge a marriage between

Kaspa and Ledger. This bond would make Romeo and Juliet's romance seem trivial.

And now, we have coderofstuff, entrusted with the arduous task of completing a captivating tale yet to have its final chapter written. The plot thickens, unexpected twists are yet to unravel, and the stakes rise as high as an overeager pole vaulter. Yet, with every stroke of his keyboard, he solves, creates, and progresses. He weaves his way through Ledger's intricate mechanics, harmonizing them with the distinctive elements of Kaspa.

Let's put on our technological spectacles and delve into the matter at hand. Imagine a bustling library, not the physical one, with towering shelves and dimly lit corners where forgotten books reside. No, envision the digital library of Kaspa, where countless transactions unfold within its well-organized blockDAG catalog. But like any thriving library, Kaspa has its limits, and one of them is memory, as fleeting as the memory of my Aunt Edna after a few brunch mimosas.

We have entities called nodes in this library, diligent librarians meticulously recording every transaction. However, these regular nodes can only retain records for three days due to Kaspa's pruning mechanism, similar to removing outdated books from the shelves. Transactions older than that are consigned to the digital archives, like aging newspaper clippings fading away in storage.

This brings us to our "archival nodes" group, the scholars in the shadows. They resemble the bookish students at a dance party, brimming with knowledge but lacking peers with whom to share it. The absence of Peer-to-Peer (P2P) communication prevents them from exchanging the normally pruned data. If this were an '80s teen movie, we would witness a montage with upbeat music and a wise mentor, and by the end, our bookworms would become kings of the dance floor. Alas, this is not an '80s teen movie.

However, our archival nodes are not left without hope. Plans are underway to implement improvements that would enable these nodes to shine and flex their memory muscles. With this upgrade, Kaspa could boast a more comprehensive block explorer that digs deep into the annals of past transactions beyond the limits of Kaspa's current pruning point.

Imagine Kaspa's personal time machine, capable of revisiting transactions from more than just three days ago. It's similar to having a knowledgeable historian who can recount past events without flipping through dusty tomes or running out of breath.

With these upgraded archival nodes, we entrust them with the role of custodians of digital history, preserving data long pruned from standard nodes. It's an opportunity for our studious nodes to take center stage. It may not be an '80s movie transformation but undeniably thrilling.

And when it's all said and done, we envision a future where our block explorer becomes an archaeologist, unearthing Kaspa's treasures from the past. No more time constraints, no more out-of-reach data. Complete, unrestricted access to Kaspa's transaction history awaits.

Smart contracts have revolutionized digital transactions. To grasp their impact, we must first understand their essence. Smart contracts are code snippets that facilitate, verify, and enforce agreements. Picture a traditional contract, such as purchasing a house. It typically involves lawyers, real estate agents, banks, and numerous other entities. Each step requires time, trust, and often significant expenses. Imagine an environment where this entire process is automated, trustless, and supremely efficient. Lose a middleman with this one simple trick.

Initiating a smart contract creates a chain reaction, like a row of falling dominos. The contract contains predefined rules, and once those conditions are met, it executes itself without any need for intermediaries. For instance, in a property sale, a smart contract can automatically transfer ownership to the buyer once the agreed-upon sum is transferred to the seller's account. It's an autonomous system that eliminates the possibility of human error, bias, or manipulation.

Rollups

While smart contracts have been transformative, more advanced technology is now taking center stage: Rollups. Just as email revolutionized traditional mail, Rollups are set to significantly enhance smart contracts and the broader crypto landscape. And yes, someone will inevitably create a Fruit Rollup contract. I'm calling it; you heard it here first.

Rollups tackle the pressing issue of scalability. Imagine a congested highway during rush hour, packed with single-passenger cars. The more cars, the slower the traffic, and the longer it takes everyone to reach their destinations. Enter Rollups, the solution to our traffic woes. They're like the meticulous Mayor in a game of SimCity, optimizing lane usage while managing spontaneous tornadoes and pesky alien invasions.

The magic of Rollups lies in their approach. Instead of each passenger (transaction) occupying its own space on the highway, Rollups bundle multiple transactions together. It's akin to replacing a fleet of private cars with high-capacity buses. Each bus accommodates numerous passengers but occupies the road space of a single vehicle.

This method drastically reduces congestion on the network highway, enabling faster and more efficient transaction processing. It's similar to introducing a fleet of buses to our rush hour scenario, expanding the overall capacity of the highway without physically expanding it. It's an innovative solution promising speed, efficiency, and fewer traffic jams in the crypto landscape.

Kaspa, already established as the world's fastest Proof-of-Work chain, gazes toward the future with eager anticipation. Always at the forefront of progress, Kaspa views the potential of Rollups with strategic interest. It doesn't merely keep pace with the crypto crowd; it leads the charge. That's what it means to be genuinely forward-thinking. Kaspa's exploration of Rollups might be the fuel that propels this rocket into an entirely new realm of influence and speed.

Some Smart Contract Options

As we peek into Kaspa's treasure trove of potential, two captivating paths unfold before us. The first path that catches our attention is the creation of native smart contracts within the boundaries of Kaspa's own ecosystem. It's kind of like upgrading from an old manual typewriter to a sleek, modern word processor with autocorrect and spell check. It's ducking fast, trustless, and efficient.

Embarking on this path involves more than adjusting a few parameters in the network. It requires delving into Kaspa's architecture and modifying its DNA, the base protocol that governs the network's operations.

This journey necessitates a hard fork, a substantial change in the network's rules that creates a new branch of the blockDAG while preserving the existing one. Implementing a hard fork is like forging a new evolutionary path, demanding careful planning, strategizing, and consensus among network participants.

Furthermore, executing this plan requires a significant investment in human resources. A team of highly skilled developers must dedicate countless hours to meticulous work, debugging, and testing to ensure the smooth operation of the new protocol.

This decision is not to be taken lightly. It requires ample time and intellectual capital. It's an effort comparable to assembling a team of geneticists to engineer a new species—complex, challenging, but potentially groundbreaking. It's not just about adding new skills or tools to Kaspa; it's about reshaping its genome to unlock new possibilities for growth and evolution.

Fortunately, Matter Labs' zkSync offers good insights and serves as an excellent reference point for modeling. Using zkSync's innovative work as a roadmap is comparable to following a Gordon Ramsay recipe to cook a five-course meal—it won't make the process effortless. Still, it's an excellent starting point.

What are the advantages of native Rollups for Kaspa? It grants Kaspa complete control. With native Rollups, Kaspa can optimize its performance according to its unique needs and potential, like a master chef fine-tuning a recipe to create a signature dish. It allows Kaspa to tailor the system to its operational rhythm, delivering an unparalleled user experience admired even by seasoned software engineers. The focus would be on Kaspa and the development of its ecosystem capabilities.

Successfully deploying this native approach could propel Kaspa from a respected player to a true blockDAG champion. It's not just about keeping up with the Kardashians of the digital world; it's about setting trends that others strive to emulate.

A second route for Kaspa's integration with Rollups revolves around leveraging Ethereum's mature DeFi (Decentralized Finance) platform. In this setup, Kaspa acts as a dispatcher, managing transaction sequencing. Ethereum, in turn, serves as the final authority, settling these transactions.

Kaspa's role in this collaboration is similar to an air traffic controller at a bustling airport, coordinating the flow of transactions (planes) to ensure efficient sequencing and settlement by Ethereum. Kaspa ensures that transactions are organized and streamlined, positioning them correctly for Ethereum's finalization, just like airplanes aligning for a safe and efficient landing.

This pathway offers a less disruptive integration, requiring minor modifications to Kaspa's existing setup compared to implementing native smart contracts. The division of labor between Kaspa and Ethereum means that Ethereum handles the bulk of settlement-related tasks. At the same time, Kaspa leverages its strengths in transaction sequencing.

To further enhance efficiency, Kaspa could leverage the shared prover technology developed by Starkware. This technology enables multiple users or transactions to share proof computation, reducing computational overhead and enhancing overall efficiency. This shared proof system acts as a turbo boost, amplifying Kaspa's sequencing capability and streamlining its integration with Ethereum.

Moreover, this approach creates opportunities for Kaspa users to engage with Ethereum's robust DeFi ecosystem. By acting as a sequencer for Ethereum, Kaspa becomes a gateway for users to access Ethereum's wide range of financial applications, further enhancing the utility and value proposition of the Kaspa network.

What's fascinating is that these two paths are not mutually exclusive. Kaspa could pursue both routes simultaneously, cultivating its native smart contracts while serving as an efficient sequencing layer for Ethereum. This dual approach expands the spectrum of possibilities for Kaspa's role and influence in the crypto space, creating a dynamic and versatile future. It fosters adoption and inclusion and offers a lifeline to struggling networks.

With the unfolding saga of blockDAG technology merging with Rollup functionality, Kaspa is carving out a unique position. It promises to become an unmissable, ever-evolving narrative worthy of attention from the world at large.

The Knight of the DAG

You find yourself seeking refuge from the rain, taking shelter in a dimly lit tavern, your hand cradling a half-filled tankard of camaraderie, a smoky blend of pipe tobacco, hearth fire, and stale spirits tingling your senses, a mysterious figure enters. The room falls into a hushed silence as the enigmatic silhouette strides forward. With a barely audible murmur, the figure announces, "Behold, the DAG KNIGHT!"

Yes, indeed, our next protagonist emerges — the DAG KNIGHT Protocol.

Curiosity piques within you, and as you ponder the question, "Wut?" your words dissipate into the frothy depths of your ale. It's a valid question, but DAG KNIGHT is a tale for another day. Rest assured, it's a narrative of immense value. Imagine a consensus protocol so agile, so resilient to Byzantine trickery, that it leaves its peers in awe, its magical essence unrivaled. It surpasses GHOSTDAG, adapting flawlessly to the network's latency landscape. Intrigued? You should be.

As the last droplets of ale slide down the sides of your tankard, a feeling of eager anticipation washes over you. What does the future hold for our gallant Kaspa, with the looming prospect of DAG KNIGHT? I won't divulge all the secrets at once, but I can offer a hint: it promises grandeur. A true game-changer. This campaign is not one to be missed.

Chapter 10

The Gallant Guardian

Ladies and gentlemen, let's get ready to rumble! In the protocol corner, preliminary challenger of the heavyweight Kaspa title, the magnificent, wondrous, and undeniably complex yet incredibly intriguing—the DAG KNIGHT protocol. Poring over the marvel that is DAG KNIGHT, one can't help but be struck by its immense complexity. It's the perfect boxing match, where the athletes are not just throwing flurries of punches, but each move is calculated, each feint is planned, and each jab and hook executed with Mike Tyson precision. Understanding and fully appreciating this advanced protocol is no mere sparring match—it's a world title fight.

The complexity isn't just for show—it's the very essence of DAG KNIGHT's strength and its ability to meet the demands of a global digital economy. It's also intimidating to write about, and I thought GHOSTDAG was rough. Sheesh. Anyway, DAG KNIGHT is just as intricate as the footwork of a boxing match, with its layers of dodges, uppercuts, and counterpunches ensuring a captivating spectacle. DAG KNIGHT's detailed structure, with its layers of K-Coloring, event sequences, rank increases, and more, provides optimized chain selection, scalability, and robust security. The challenge lies not in getting knocked out by these technical details but instead appreciating the remarkable strategy and skill that powers the entire system.

It's undeniable—DAG KNIGHT carries with it ingenious potential. It stands as an advanced and complex system that pushes the boundaries of what we once thought was possible. Just as a title fight carries the potential to change the boxing world, DAG KNIGHT could redefine the world of decentralized networks.

Sounds intense, right? It is. In fact, to the uninitiated, it's about as bewildering as trying to decipher why your cat insists on crying for more food with a full food bowl or why avocados refuse to ripen until that one moment you're not looking, then decide to go from rock hard to a squishy mess. But here we are, embarking on this seemingly insurmountable journey of comprehending the DAG KNIGHT protocol together. It's quite the challenge, but let's dive in anyway, like the curious gluttons for ~~punishment~~ knowledge seekers that we are.

BlockDAG 2.0

Beneath its elaborate façade lies a novel concept that could change our thoughts about cryptocurrency technology. And though it might initially seem as inscrutable as a last-minute tax form or as cryptic as interpreting what your tenth-grade English teacher thinks Shakespeare really means, the DAG KNIGHT protocol is a wonder to behold once comprehended.

Alright, let's get medieval on ourselves and discuss the DAG KNIGHT protocol. It's like a captivating game of chess where you're tempted to open with the French Defense, but let's be honest, chess isn't everyone's cup of tea, and even I don't know what the French Defense means, yet I'm writing about it. With its abundance of pieces and intricate rules, it can seem overwhelming and time-consuming to master. However, once you delve into it and start understanding the intricacies, you'll realize that it's actually a rewarding and enjoyable game.

The digital currency and blockchain technology world has evolved faster than the few minutes of LaserDisc to DVD. Yet, we've hit a plateau. Existing protocols have done their part, like dutiful office workers clocking in, day in and day out. But just like that cookie-cutter office worker dreaming of a promotion yet not ambitious enough to get that raise, these protocols have limitations and a lack of creativity, which impedes them from making it to the big leagues of finance.

This is where our DAG KNIGHT in shining armor rides in on a protocol steed. DAG KNIGHT is like that guy who shows up to a dodgeball tournament and takes gym class hero to the next level. It's got this spark, this potential, just aching to completely transform how we approach distributed ledgers.

In the heart of DAG KNIGHT beats the concept of K-Coloring. 'K-Colouring' is the actual terminology used, but I refuse to spell it all weird with a 'u.' That's right, Yonatan and Michael, I refuse! This brings me to my next point, the authors of this masterpiece are the fabled Yonatan Sompolinsky and the brilliant Michael Sutton.

K-coloring is something like a master codebreaker's strategy for cracking a secret message. Instead of spy letters, we're talking about efficiently ordering transactions on a distributed ledger. It's the fine art of synchronization and arrangement, making the cogs of this intricate machine run smoothly.

But it's not just about coloring inside the lines (which is impossible, by the way). DAG KNIGHT takes it a step further with the concept of event sequences and rank increases. Now, I know that sounds like the stuff of dry history textbooks. But in reality, it's the pulse of this protocol, the mechanism that gives it life and functionality. A director's cut edition of a movie. You get the sequence of scenes, but you also see the layers, the depth, and the details that add richness and make the story genuinely captivating.

Returning to the K-Coloring algorithm offers a unique perspective that diverges from traditional notions of serenity and tranquility. Rather than envisioning intricate designs or patterns, let's explore it as a process of contemplation and data. It operates recursively, much like a series of interconnected ideas that unfold one after another, revealing more profound layers of intricacy and complexity.

In the case of K-Coloring, it keeps calling itself, again and again, arranging data into an efficient, elegant structure. At the core of this is the concept of research. Imagine it as the algorithm's own in-built GPS. When switched on, the algorithm freely hunts around, finding the most efficient path to arrange the transactions. A bit like looking for the shortest line in a Walmart, except it's looking for the most efficient way to place a new piece of data.

Next, we've got the event sequence denoted as Et,Z. No, it's not a new Star Wars droid, but it is just as cool. It's like the rules that the K-Coloring algorithm follows to color each block. This sequence helps decide when to color a block and when to skip it, much like a poker game dictating when you play and when to fold.

Unlike DAG KNIGHT, the current protocol GHOSTDAG is designed to optimize block selection in a blockchain environment. GHOSTDAG utilizes a system of block selection based on the heaviest subtree within the blockchain. While efficient in its own right, this weight-based approach does not possess the recursive or strategic coloring element found in the DAG KNIGHT protocol.

In GHOSTDAG, the sequence of block arrangement is more straightforward. It adheres to the general principle of favoring heavier sub-graphs instead of the event sequence-based strategy found in DAG KNIGHT. Hence, while GHOSTDAG excels at optimizing block selection in specific scenarios, it lacks the nuanced coloring approach and strategic block placement that sets DAG KNIGHT apart. The difference in watching TV in black & white versus color. Chocolate syrup for blood will no longer fly on today's television.

When 'free_search' is true, the algorithm doesn't start breaking the rules or validating invalid transactions. Instead, it changes how it navigates through the data. It's like deciding to take a different path through a maze because it might be quicker, rather than always sticking to the same route. For example, it might choose to process certain groups of transactions out of the standard order if it determines that doing so will be more efficient.

This doesn't mean the protocol suddenly becomes an anarchic free-for-all. All transactions are still validated according to the network's rules, and any invalid transactions are rejected. The security of the system remains intact.

In contrast, the GHOSTDAG protocol lacks this level of flexibility and adaptability. Its operation follows a predetermined set of rules, like a traditional egg-spoon relay race with runners strictly adhering to their lanes, cautious and calculated. While this approach provides its own set of advantages regarding consistency, it doesn't offer the same level of dynamism as DAG KNIGHT's adaptive 'free_search' feature.

Lastly, we've got the concept of a rank increase. It sounds like a promotion, and it's not far off. In the DAG KNIGHT protocol hierarchy, a block's rank indicates its position and importance. An increase in rank is like a VIP pass—it allows for a block to have a more significant role in the structure. It's like if you've been working in the mailroom and suddenly you're called to attend the board meeting.

GHOSTDAG operates more on the principle of 'weight' instead of 'rank.' Rather than promoting blocks based on a hierarchical rank, its system favors those with the 'heaviest' transactional value, thereby lacking the nuanced ranking approach found in DAG KNIGHT.

Onward to scalability, it's a finicky hiccup in crypto, a system built to overturn how we handle transactions. However, it's a reality that we can no longer ignore. Here we are at a fast-food drive-thru that, due to popularity, can't serve its customers quickly anymore. The replacement for fiat, known as Bitcoin, has transaction times starting at ten minutes and up. The long lines and wait times detract from the experience, and this, in a nutshell, is the scalability problem that all traditional blockchains face. As transaction volumes grow, so do the processing times, and users are left twiddling their thumbs. Not great for a 'fast food' business model, Mister Nakamoto.

Here's where DAG KNIGHT rides to the rescue. Not that GHOSTDAG wasn't at the scene first, but everyone is a sucker for the knight in shining armor. It's not just a new way to handle transactions; it's a game-changer that pushes the boundaries of what we thought was possible. DAG KNIGHT employs a strategic approach that might be more comparable to self-checkout lanes in the drive-thru. It allows for multiple blocks of transactions to be processed simultaneously. The technical term for this is parallelization, and it's one of the reasons why GHOSTDAG has turned heads in the industry.

On top of parallelization, DAG KNIGHT utilizes an optimized chain selection mechanism that can be likened to one of those insanely skillful video game speedrunners. It strategically selects the transactions that contribute most to the network's security and efficiency, providing an extra layer of optimization to the process.

Parameterless

Understanding the concept of 'parameterless' may seem somewhat elusive, so let's break it down using a straightforward, daily life example without falling back on more math and techs. Parameters are like the recipe you follow for baking a cake. Generally, you need to adhere to a specific sequence, using particular ingredients in certain quantities and baking at just the right temperature and time. These directions represent the 'parameters' that navigate how you bake the cake.

Coincidentally, in our cake and in the world of coding, these parameters often boil down to numbers. For instance, in our cake recipe, "preheat the oven to 350 degrees Fahrenheit," "2 cups of flour," or "3 large eggs." We follow these parameters to achieve the desired triple chocolate cakeDAG protocol. Veer off these numbers, and you might end up with something resembling a binary brick rather than a cake.

The same goes for blockchain protocols. Here, the numbers get mixed in a bit with hieroglyphics—an upper bound on delay (D),

Bitcoin's block creation rate ($\lambda = 1/600$ blocks/sec), or PHANTOM's k—they dictate the system's operation and outcomes nonetheless. These parameters must be met to validate a block of transactions.

In contrast, a 'parameterless' approach is like being handed all the ingredients to bake a cake without any strict recipe. You have the liberty to mix and match the ingredients as you wish, adjusting them according to your preference. Suppose you discover a novel, efficient method to boil a cake in an air fryer to achieve the desired results. In that case, you are entirely free to pursue it. Probably shouldn't, but I'm not your parameter.

DAG KNIGHT vs Protocols
Bringing this back to protocols; traditional cryptocurrencies like Bitcoin have these ironclad rules in place, similar to our recipe. They stick to specifics, like block size or the time between blocks, ruling their operation with a steady, unchanging hand. But why is it so rigid? It's their safety blanket, ensuring predictability and stability in varying network conditions. These parameters are great for playing it safe, but at the cost of adaptability to changing network conditions.

Enter DAG KNIGHT, the rebel of the traditional protocols, flaunting its 'parameterless' badge with pride. When it comes to dealing with network latency, this guy doesn't play by the rules, mainly because it doesn't have any set rules.

This isn't some kind of crypto-anarchist; DAG KNIGHT still has a set goal and procedures. Though, now it has the freedom to figure out what works best for latency. Yep, being parameterless means that DAG KNIGHT self-adapts and fine-tunes its operation to the rhythm of the network, unrestrained by the chains of pre-set norms. It's like it has its fingers on the pulse of the network, reading the optimal pace of operation. This slick adaptability allows DAG KNIGHT to strut its stuff more efficiently and effectively, regardless of the mood swings of network conditions.

The result of this flexibility is that DAG KNIGHT has the potential to significantly outperform traditional blockchain protocols. It's like shopping for wall paint and discovering you can remove your sunglasses. You had them on to protect your eyes from a nuclear fusion reactor in the sky, but, at this moment, you don't need them in the hardware store. DAG KNIGHT does similarly, pioneering this new approach in the blockchain world, pushing the boundaries of efficiency, speed, and adaptability. This revolutionary approach is not just about resolving existing limitations but also evolving with infrastructure as it advances. So, in the future, when the Internet runs even faster, DAG KNIGHT can speed up with it.

Security is a significant concern for any system handling sensitive transactions and data, and always at the forefront of any crypto's design. When it comes to finances, it's akin to trying to keep the peace in a room full of luchadors with something to prove; it's challenging but necessary. And when it comes to DAG KNIGHT, some nifty mechanisms are in place to ensure the integrity of the network.

DAG KNIGHT vs GHOSTDAG

Let's revisit K-Coloring, the central component of DAG KNIGHT. It's a familiar beast from GHOSTDAG but operates differently here. Think of it as the supervisor on a building site, ensuring every worker (or block, in our case) knows their role and doesn't stray into another's territory. It allocates each block's unique identification, nipping any potential conflicts in the bud. A construction worker accidentally drills a hole where the unknowing electrician is installing wiring. Did somebody say OSHA? K-Coloring ensures it won't happen, as a supervisor guides them with a living, adaptable blueprint.

And here comes a term that might have you thinking we've veered into sci-fi territory: reorg. It's not a cyborg or an alien species but operates with similar precision. Consider reorg as the ever-vigilant foreman, ensuring every task is up to standard. It reviews the blocks, and if any are found slacking or pulling any tricks, it flags them for inspection.

Contrasting GHOSTDAG with DAG KNIGHT, it's like comparing an old-school hammer and chisel to modern laser-guided carving tools. They're both accomplishing the same goal, but the precision, speed, and sophistication are worlds apart. K-Coloring isn't just keeping the peace among blocks; it's the laser-guided system ensuring the network's smooth, efficient, and orderly functioning.

Within the construction project, DAG KNIGHT, K-Coloring, and reorg are the diligent overseers ensuring everyone plays by the rules, maximizes productivity, and keeps mishaps at bay. They're the foundation, the base layer under the protocol to make this architectural marvel stand firm.

Now, let's talk about 'bursts.' Remember the whole Starburst thing from GHOSTDAG? You probably don't; it was a lame joke. Anyway, bursts act much like earthquakes do in the natural world. In geological terms, earthquakes are unexpected and sudden, drastically shaking things up—quite literally.

In the same way, bursts add an unpredictable element to the network by introducing random blocks. These sudden shifts in the block landscape make it far more challenging for any would-be fraudsters to predict the system and manipulate it to their advantage. It's as if DAG KNIGHT has its very own tectonic controls built in, constantly keeping the network on its toes. So, in this seismic landscape, you better keep your transactions honest or be prepared for the ground to shake beneath your feet.

Chain selection is another significant factor that contributes to the security of DAG KNIGHT. It's a bit like a democratic election where everyone gets a fair shot, and the best candidate is chosen. In DAG KNIGHT, this process is automated to ensure the most optimized and secure chain is always selected. This prevents any one node from dominating the network and maintains a level of fairness that's crucial in a decentralized system.

It's clear that DAG KNIGHT takes security seriously, utilizing various innovative methods to ensure the safety of transactions and the integrity of the network. From K-Coloring and reorgs to bursts and chain selection, every aspect of DAG KNIGHT's security mechanism works harmoniously to fend off potential threats and maintain a secure, efficient, and fair network for all users. The result is a protocol that's not just powerful and efficient but also one of the safest algorithms in the world of cryptocurrency. It's not just a new protocol; it's a financial revolution in the making.

DAG KNIGHT's potential ramifications go beyond just being a new kid on the cryptocurrency block. It's more like a powerful wave that could bring about dramatic shifts in how we conduct financial transactions, opening up fascinating possibilities that were only a pipedream in the pre-DAG KNIGHT era.

DAG KNIGHT in Practice
One of the most immediate impacts of DAG KNIGHT could be seen in financial transactions.

With its superior processing speed, ramped-up security, and lowered costs, DAG KNIGHT is set to give the traditional banking system a 'bank run' for its money. It's like upgrading from a telegraph to the information transfer capabilities of high-speed Internet—the difference is that stark. Transactions that once took hours or even days could be settled in near real-time. Not only is DAG KNIGHT as fast as the Internet, but it's making the waiting game, security threats, conversion rate loss, and middlemen a thing of the past.

For everyday users, this increased efficiency could translate to a more seamless use of digital currencies on the Kaspa network. Imagine paying for your morning newspaper or monthly utilities with KAS as quickly as you'd use your credit card with instant settlement, removing the fear of the transactions settling days later or keeping track of receipts and other needless wastes of energy. It's not just about being a techy, futuristic way of paying. It's about making digital currencies more than just a niche and something as commonplace and accepted as our regular fiat currencies.

So, if we crank this all the way up to the macro level, we'll see how financial institutions might just be the biggest cheerleaders for DAG KNIGHT. We're talking about a sector where the holy trinity is security, speed, and cost-effectiveness. It may be a snoozefest for most everyday folks, but when you get it right, it's like making a perfect hangover breakfast on Sunday morning—an absolute game-changer, maybe even a lifesaver.

DAG KNIGHT could be the ultimate platform for the ultimate tax software that not only rapidly calculates your liabilities and deductions with precision but instantly finds and rectifies discrepancies in your previous returns. Imagine how valuable that would be for the businesses that crash under the weight of an Excel spreadsheet. That's what we call an optimized operation and cost-saving. Tax season just became less daunting, didn't it?

And then there's the bustling, breakneck world of e-commerce. When you're ready to check out your online cart, you know the feeling, but the payment process will take a thousand passwords and hundreds of cards, so you abandon it. Well, DAG KNIGHT could be the anesthetic for that pain. Swapping a sluggish, rusty shopping cart for a sweet hoverboard, your online shopping experience becomes faster, smoother, and over in a flash. And for the businesses, it's a clear win. No more grimacing at the sight of abandoned carts and missed opportunities.

It's no overstatement to say that the potential implications and benefits of DAG KNIGHT are immense. From individual users to big corporations, the ripples of this technological innovation could touch every corner of our digital world. It has the potential to redefine financial transactions, making them faster, cheaper, and safer, thus paving the way for a more accessible and efficient digital economy. It's not just about creating a new cryptocurrency protocol; it's about ushering in a new era where digital currencies are an integral part of our everyday lives. And with DAG KNIGHT, that future seems more achievable than ever.

Complex, Yet Satisfying

Poring over the marvel that is DAG KNIGHT, one can't help but be struck by its immense complexity. Much like attempting to crochet a Beanie Baby blindfolded or pulling off a 3D-printed Lamborghini in your garage, understanding and fully appreciating this advanced protocol is no cakewalk. Yet, the complexity isn't just for show—it's the very essence of DAG KNIGHT's strength and its ability to meet the demands of a global digital economy.

The intricate mechanisms that ensure precision and accuracy, DAG KNIGHT's detailed structure, with its layers of K-Coloring, event sequences, rank increases, and more, provides optimized chain selection, scalability, and robust security. The challenge lies in not becoming overwhelmed by these technical details but appreciating the great engine under the hood that powers the entire system. After all, it took years of work to dream up; it's only fair that it would take a hefty amount of time to understand.

Encouragingly, while the initial learning curve might seem steep, the journey to understanding DAG KNIGHT can be immensely rewarding. Just as one wouldn't give up on attempting to understand quantum physics after reading a Wikipedia article, coming to grips with DAG KNIGHT requires patience, persistence, and a thirst for exploration. The key is to remember that each technical jargon, every concept, and all the intricate details combine to form a masterpiece that could redefine how we understand and use cryptocurrencies.

It's undeniable—DAG KNIGHT carries with it a revolutionary potential. Just as the Internet transformed our world at the end of the last century,

DAG KNIGHT could very well alter the world of decentralized networks in this century. It's not a far-fetched claim or exaggerated hype—it's a real possibility, and the signs are all around us. From improving financial transactions to making digital currencies more accessible, the implications are vast and exciting.

DAG KNIGHT carries within it the continued solution of the blockchain trilemma of decentralization, security, and scalability. Seamlessly melding these three aspects paves the way for a more efficient and secure digital future. Only now, by lifting one of the few remaining limitations of parameters for latency. It's a future where transactions are swift, security is robust, and the potential for scalability is no longer a distant dream but a realized reality.

DAG KNIGHT is a demonstration of human ingenuity and the relentless pursuit of innovation. It pushes the boundaries of blockchain technology and brings us one step closer to a world where digital currencies are not just an alternative but a mainstream/ method of transaction.

Chapter 11

A Canopy Solution for a Root Problem

In the electrifying stage play of cryptocurrency, where the script isn't written beforehand, the performers improvise in confusion, and the drama is probably the whole production itself. There's no room for extras idling in the backdrop or the diva that can't carry a tune. Every character is a scene-stealer, a theatrical force of chaos that captivates the ever-evolving, diverse audience.

Cue in Kaspa, our leading lady, who entered on screen equipped with a rapid-fire emission rate, a fast network speed, and a compelling character arc designed to unfold entirely within our own act. It emerged not from burned-out auditions but from a hotbed of innovation, its persona sculpted with a high-tech code so masterful it'd leave Turing starstruck.

You see, all this dramatic flourish, this riveting story arc doesn't amount to much if there's no audience to witness it. An unopened script, however profound or hard-hitting, is just a bunch of words if left in a drawer to collect dust.

And what happens when we reach the most anticipated moment—the climactic bull market scene where the prices dramatically rise and, surprise, surprise, predictably fall? What's the community's next act? Do we just sit idle, twiddling our thumbs, hoping that some benevolent foundation, heroic venture capitalist, or centralized entity swoops in with a happy ending? Don't bet on it.

Kaspa's timeline features some pretty snazzy events—a rewrite to the Rust codebase, DAG KNIGHT, and smart contracts. But are we supposed to simply wait for these advancements to manifest and then bemoan their underutilization as we desperately scramble for developers? It's like producing a high-budget film, hosting a premiere, and then, oops, forgetting to advertise.

Right now, Kaspa is akin to an enormous stage with a lone performer. It's like having a theater that can hold thousands, but there's only one actor on the scene and a single spectator in the audience. The release of Rust is like expanding the theater size, but we're still stuck with one performer and one spectator.

We need a solution that not only anticipates these advancements but actively prepares for them, amplifying their strengths and proudly presenting them to the world. We can't be passive, reacting only after these features are released. We must actively search for developers for the network and the ecosystem and promote adoption among institutions and retail.

This isn't about rushing to the end or spoiling the grand finale, either. It's about crafting a story that captivates the audience and has them on the edge of their seats, eagerly anticipating the narrative.

So, the real question isn't "What's next?" but "How do we make 'what's next' a blockbuster?" Because the success of the Kaspa saga isn't determined by some centralized entity where we can cheer for it from the sidelines. It's on us—all of us—to step up and take action. It's the community's responsibility to act now, learn from the past, and prepare for the future. This is what community governance means.

Technologically and theoretically, Kaspa is a near masterpiece. But when it comes to developers, merchants, student interns, dApps, DeFi, and users, we're lacking. We need all of these things. As well as adoption, sustainability, and to be a currency! Kaspa's designed to function as digital cash, but at present, and in the immediate future, it seems we're more like a penny stock. The drama's only just begun, making a Saturday night with TheSheepcat and KaffinPX look boring.

I know what's probably whirring through your mind as I gear up to reveal my store-brand thesis. But before we get there, let's lay some groundwork. My journey with Kaspa began and still dwells in education. That's where my passion began and my initial motive. I've since found myself wearing an assortment of hats, a Jack-of-all-trades yet master of none.

Sure, it may seem like I have a role I favor, but that's more a matter of what you see rather than where my loyalties lie. My roles are like the planets of our solar system. They might vary in size and visibility from Earth, but that doesn't change the fact that they all revolve around the same sun—my dedication to Kaspa.

Here comes my solution and suggestion, which might differ from what you'd expect, or it might be everything you'd expect. I suppose it's what role you know me for. If you know me at all.

Marketing

Yes, marketing. I know the dreaded m-word that screams centralized corporate capitalist propaganda. It paints a picture of internet pop ups, tabloids, and the excellent series with a terrible ending known as Mad Men. Marketing is the cure-all to our current ailments. And no, that's not my PR persona speaking, nor is it a bias from the array of any other role that I've played. This is my sincere analysis and the conclusion I've reached through, what I think, is careful examination.

Marketing Kaspa is not a superficial facade but a critical bridge linking Kaspa's innovative technologies with those who benefit from them. It's the key to unlocking our potential, moving from underutilization to a sustainable and stable network to full capacity. Surfacing from meme-coin sea level to a recognized ranking on the summit of crypto Mt. Everest.

Just as the Bitcoin of yesteryears couldn't grow in the shadows, Kaspa cannot rely solely on the inherent strengths of its brilliance and hope for miraculous growth. Bitcoin might have enjoyed the leisure of slow, steady growth and gained notoriety while never becoming more than a prototype. Kaspa, however, is built for a different breed and era of competitive finance. And competition is at an all-time high and set for another breakout. Kaspa is not merely looking to participate in the crypto race; it aims to outrun, outshine, and outlast. Treating Kaspa any other way is an injustice. Much like the speed of the network bolsters the security of the blockDAG, the haste of adoption will shore up the reality that Kaspa can't be denied.

This is where the importance of marketing becomes glaringly evident. Marketing for Kaspa isn't about creating buy-and-sell pressure; it's about awareness and utilizing a tool inextricably linked with the ethos of proof-of-work cryptocurrency—game theory.

Fun for the Whole Family
Game theory, the foundation of crypto, is about making strategic decisions and fundamentally explores how an optimal outcome often arises when individuals strategize for personal gain and consider the collective benefit. This tends to create the most

advantageous scenario for themselves and a group as a whole.

Consider the example of Kaspa mining, the virtual gold rush where individual miners or mining pools compete to solve complex computational puzzles to validate transactions and add them to the blockDAG. This, in turn, earns them a reward, typically in the form of the KAS. While chasing personal gains in the form of these rewards simultaneously, they contribute to the overall health and security of the network. Their efforts validate transactions, ensuring the integrity and trustworthiness of the system. Hence, their personal gain translates into a collective victory—the strength of the blockDAG.

The same game theory applies when we invest and contribute to marketing Kaspa. It's not just moving a pawn forward; it's setting the stage for a checkmate. Carving a path to help Kaspa leap over the competition makes it the equivalent of a crypto rook, darting unhindered across the board. By driving marketing, recruiting, educating, and generating awareness, we create demand for Kaspa and push for further adoption. And if you made it this far into my book or even have a smidge of market knowledge, you know what increased demand does for price action. It's a strategy that benefits both the collective and the individual. Game theory.

GRO

While grassroots and organic (GRO, let's make this a thing) marketing is well suited for Kaspa's user base and ethos, these techniques offer diminishing returns in the vacuum of social media echo chambers. To make a significant impact, we need to back these efforts with both financial and manpower resources. Thus, the need to embark on a journey to delve deeper into Kaspa's marketing strategies, community engagement efforts, and crucial governance model enhancements.

Cryptocurrency marketing has an even more crucial role than in traditional business landscapes. This is a sphere where the next big thing is always just around the corner and where audiences are notoriously fickle, hopping from one promising coin to another. Against such a backdrop, strategic marketing isn't just a nice-to-have. It's a downright survival necessity.

Bitcoin, often seen as the progenitor of the crypto landscape, has been able to coast along its trajectory primarily due to the advantage of being first to the party. Yet, its snail-paced evolution and increasingly glaring shortcomings present a ripe opportunity for younger, more agile cryptocurrencies like Kaspa to stake their claim. However, a robust and well-funded marketing strategy is imperative to convert this opportunity into substantial growth. And I'm not talking about the strung-out shoestring budget of the Community Marketing Fund. We need a solid, stable, and sustainable allowance and plan. Otherwise, we're allowing another more competitive network the opportunity to slide into Kaspa's rightful place.

Kaspa has everything going for it except for this area of competitiveness. Without capitalizing on Kaspa's momentum and maintaining escape velocity, the real threat to this ingenious technological solution is becoming a ghost chain, turning into a hyper-efficient skeletal network of promises and zero use.

Yeah, yeah, "BuT BiTcOiN hAd DeCeNtRaLiZeD oRgAnIc GrOwTh." Bitcoin was also the first and only competition-less crypto, as well. Not only is this argument not valid or applicable to Kaspa, but organic growth and GRO marketing also aren't two different species; they're two sides of the same leaf. Organic growth carries an authenticity that builds trust, akin to a sturdy tree taking root. With its educational and supportive nature, GRO marketing is like a tree's branches reaching out, spreading its influence and touching places the trunk alone can't reach.

The crypto ecosystem, much like a natural forest, treasures the principles of decentralization and grassroots movements. It's a wild, untamed woodland, where strategy and proactive efforts till the soil and shape its evolution and growth.

Consequently, it's not enough for Kaspa to grow in this forest. It must stand tall above the canopy, letting the world notice its vibrant foliage. Kaspa must showcase its unique features, such as its state-of-the-art code, fast transactions, and swift lifecycle to full effect, much like a rare species of tree exhibiting its striking leaves. Furthermore, it implies ensuring that the tree's distinctive attributes are clearly visible and compelling and remain consistent throughout the seasons, converting onlookers into gardeners and these gardeners into ardent caretakers.

In essence, we aren't choosing between organic growth and marketing. We're merging them, embracing a unified approach that aligns with the competitive yet cooperative ecosystem of the crypto garden. Only through this can Kaspa establish a strong presence in the crypto landscape, evolving from just another seedling to a remarkable tree in the heart of the digital currency forest.

We must look beyond the comforts of centralized norms and move toward a more assertive, strategic approach that aligns with the competitive and cooperative nature of the crypto industry. Only by doing so can Kaspa carve out a significant place on the finance map, becoming not just another ghost chain but a formidable player in the digital currency revolution.

The driving spirit of cryptocurrency is decentralization—distributing power and control away from a central authority and placing it in the hands of the users themselves. This decentralization is at the heart of Kaspa's design. However, there is a fine line that needs to be walked here. While the current decision-making processes tend to boil down to the guidance of the core developers, this is neither sustainable nor genuinely decentralized.

Cryptocurrency might be a digital entity, but its backbone is formed by these on-chain developers who work diligently day and night. These developers are the builders, the architects of the crypto landscape, taking abstract concepts and translating them into practical, usable tech. For Kaspa, marketing to on-chain developers is about developing redundancy, fostering understanding, and cementing security within the Kaspa codebase.

But how do you market to a group whose language is lines of code and whose currency are innovation and efficiency? You start by showcasing what sets Kaspa apart. In this case, the open sandbox of the Rust codebase and the high-tech code that powers Kaspa's operations. The problem, however, is that complexity can often be a barrier. A complex codebase might be a developer's dream, but it can also be overwhelming. Hence, our marketing strategy should highlight Kaspa's innovative features and aim to demystify them and welcome newcomers. Like a virtual reality Statue of Liberty, "Give me your tired, your poor, Your developer masses yearning to breathe creativity through code."

Eating syntax for breakfast and variables for dinner, on-chain developers navigate the digital labyrinth of Kaspa as quickly as you can navigate your favorite supermarket. And it's through platforms like webinars, boot camps, and workshops that they train, gathering wisdom on the wily ways of the Kaspa beast. It's about more than just geeking out on the next code sprint. It's about ensuring Kaspa's cryptocurrency is tighter than leather pants and more resilient than a cockroach at a nuclear test site.

Borrowing a page from nature, fortuity in the repeated understanding of the codebase strengthens the survival of the fittest. The more developers we have able to decode Kaspa's genetic blueprint, the sturdier our fortress is against wannabe invaders and time. Our mission is not just to lure on-chain developers into the club but also to transform them into gurus of the Kaspa way, the guardians of our digital castle.

While on-chain developers form the backbone of Kaspa, ecosystem developers are its lifeblood. They are the creators who will flesh out the skeletal framework provided by the on-chain developers, populating Kaspa's world with many applications and innovations. As such, our GRO strategy should also consider marketing for ecosystem developers.

With the Rust codebase, Kaspa's sporting the latest fashion in the world of code. Rust is all the rage these days, known for being as robust as a tank yet as agile as Wolfie's fat cat. However, moving to a new codebase can feel like you've just landed on Mars and the aliens are speaking in clicks and whistles. So, our job isn't just to sell these brave devs on Rust's glitz and glamor. We've also got to show them the benefits, the opportunity, and display our needs, to make their journey into Rust as smooth as something, well… not Rusty.

For the ecosystem developers, there's a golden ticket hidden within the chaos of the crypto world. An opportunity to capitalize as founders on the cutting edge of tech, shaping Kaspa's trajectory like trailblazers of old. The world's your oyster, and with early adoption, you get to pick the pearls.

Our goal here is to create a playground for these devs. A space that sparks creativity fosters innovation. Our success hinges not just on promoting Kaspa's shiny new toys but also on revealing the treasure trove that awaits in the future. If we can do that, we'll do more than just rope in developers. We'll turn them into die-hard loyalists, devout followers of the Kaspa creed.

Academics

Now let's switch gears and talk about an avenue with great potential that often is forgotten: academia. Universities and research institutions are home to some of the brightest minds. These are individuals driven by curiosity, the desire to understand the world around them, and to create solutions to problems that can change that world.

They're starting their adult lives full of vigor and dreams. And on a ramen and beer budget.

Academia, especially disciplines focused on technology and economy, can offer valuable insights into the practical and theoretical aspects of Kaspa and crypto technology. Their research could lead to innovation, improvements, or entirely new uses for the technology. However, this potential remains largely untapped and unwelcome.

To effectively engage academia, we must first create awareness about Kaspa and its research opportunities. This requires not just traditional marketing but targeted academic outreach. We need to communicate the unique problems and questions that Kaspa is tackling and the issues that could make for exciting dissertations or groundbreaking research papers.

We can even establish relationships with academic institutions for a trickle-down Reagan effect, yet successful this time. This could involve creating partnerships for research, offering grants and scholarships, or creating internship opportunities. We need to make academia feel involved and invested in the progress of Kaspa.

Finally, we need to be open to feedback and findings from academic research. This may challenge our assumptions or critique our methods. However, it's essential to remember that such feedback, while it may be tough to swallow at times, can lead to significant improvements and innovation.

Academia holds a wellspring of potential that Kaspa can benefit from. By actively engaging with academic institutions and individuals, we can facilitate a symbiotic relationship where research drives the growth and evolution of Kaspa, and Kaspa offers fertile ground for intellectual exploration. Engaging academia, like reaching out to CollegeDAO, is not just about marketing; it's about weaving Kaspa into the fabric of ongoing academic discourse and research. This is the key to unlocking long-term, sustainable growth and innovation.

As the good ship Kaspa sails on the choppy seas of crypto, her crew is a motley assembly of deckhands, swabbies, and officers, each hailing from different corners of the globe, bringing a dash of their own views to the muster. And it's this diversity that's the strength of our Kaspa hull. The swashbuckling banter keeps things interesting, filling the sails of innovation, progress, and growth.

Sure, it's not all rainbows and unicorns at times. You cram enough differing opinions into one space, and you're bound to see some fireworks. It's like a Thanksgiving dinner where everyone has different ideas about carving the turkey or politics... yuck. But you know what? If we handle our disagreements respectfully and argue like civilized adults and not like NFT monkey degens, we might just learn something. Our solutions will be sharper, and our understanding of each other deeper.

Of course, to make this work, we need to create a safe haven where everyone feels comfortable enough to spitball their wild and crazy ideas. And we're on it. We've been rolling out new communication and behavior guidelines. Plus, we're actively taking the trash out, weeding out the toxic elements to keep things clean and green.

Education is Inclusivity

For the fresh faces in the community, we're offering a welcome package loaded with tutorials, educational materials, and what I like to call the GRO survival kit. The aim? To arm every member with the tools they need to navigate the stormy seas of our community, no matter if they're a greenhorn or an old salt.

But inclusivity isn't just about leaving the front door open and hoping for the best. It's about recognizing and appreciating everyone who shows up and brings something to the table. It's about looking at each contributing individual that brings value and stating, "You matter; you make a difference." We want to breed GRO programs in our backyard and dangle a shiny carrot to encourage our members to make meaningful contributions.

And let's not forget accessibility. In our quest for inclusivity, we're pulling out all stops to ensure that everyone can climb aboard the Kaspa ship, whether they're tech wizards or technophobes, fluent in English or communicating in tongues. We're talking about multilingual resources, websites that don't need a magnifying glass to read, and support that won't make you feel like a dummy for asking 'stupid' questions.

Building an inclusive environment isn't something you can set and forget like a pot roast. It takes work, commitment, and a whole lot of elbow grease. But the reward—a lively, colorful, and engaged community—is well worth the sweat. And with the GRO program strategies in our toolkit, we're not just shooting for the moon; we're building a rocket to get us to the stars.

All We Have is Ourselves

As we continue to navigate this complex landscape, self-policing within the community is an imperative we can't ignore. As the adage goes, "With great power comes great responsibility." With the decentralization power afforded by the Kaspa network, this responsibility falls squarely on the shoulders of our community members.

The community isn't just a group of passive observers in this landscape; instead, they are active contributors to the governance and maintenance of the Kaspa network. They play an instrumental role in maintaining ethical standards, identifying and addressing discrepancies, and fostering a spirit of transparency and accountability.

The group of dedicated Kaspa community members is not just wielding a cape of protection but also a mighty shield of responsibility. I'm not talking about internet police chasing after every rule-breaker and keyboard warrior. Nope. Self-policing. It's more like running a neighborhood watch. It's about brewing a fresh batch of honesty, transparency, and mutual respect, then handing it out to everyone in the community.

We all want to live in a place where we don't need to check if we still have our wallets after a handshake. That's what we aim for in our network. In this space, everyone looks out for each other, folks hold each other accountable, not like a headmaster with a ruler but like friends sharing a common goal.

How do we bring this utopia to life? One way is to crack open the champagne and toast the members doing their bit for the community. The ones who are not just solving problems and dropping knowledge bombs but also keeping the peace and ensuring the community runs like a well-oiled... network?

Everyone in the Kaspa playground is a VIP, every action echoes throughout the network. We're all in this together, like a high school musical but with fewer jazz hands and more CLI mysticism. So, celebrating the good guys sends a message: good behavior isn't just appreciated; it's applauded. And who doesn't like a bit of applause, right?

A self-policing culture empowers community members to take ownership of the Kaspa network's health and well-being. It turns the community into an active defense line against potential threats, making it more resilient and robust. And ultimately, it ensures that the power of governance stays where it truly belongs—in the hands of the people who make up the Kaspa community. Also, I've never been a mod for real until Kaspa, but this really helps. A lot.

Is GRO the Key for Success?

Programming the course for Kaspa's future, pulling levers and pressing buttons on things like GRO marketing, developer ecosystems, schmoozing with the academics, tweaking governance, and ensuring our community's as inclusive as a pickup game of dodgeball, and you know what? It's not just a solo show. It's a full-on congregation where everyone is dedicated to the cause. And even if this take is a smidge flawed, everyone is definitely attached to price action and value. It's not hard to see the endless avenues and streets that GRO marketing can take. It's an overarching solution to most of the community's identifiable troubles.

It's the misunderstood metric of our mission. The dark matter of our galaxy. An underserved and underutilized service to ourselves. It could be an actual perpetual motion machine where the collective input would yield far larger, even massive outputs. It's something to at least consider and chew on. For real, though, actually picture it in action.

Once again, this is just my take from a viewpoint of a wide-angle shot as broad as I can fathom with my tiny drop of gray matter.

Chapter 12

You're Here Early

Kaspa is not just another cryptocurrency. It's not just another technology. It's not just another community. It's an ecosystem, a living, breathing creature woven together by the unique interplay of each of its parts. Kaspa is here for the everyday and every person, with the bold ambition to redefine finance as we know it.

The GHOSTDAG protocol, Kaspa's high school crush, is anything but ghostly. Instead, it's as tangible as that 'ding' on your phone whenever you get a like on your latest duckface selfie. It's busy handling everyday transactions, from impulse online buys (all the books I needed but will never read) to colossal institutional transfers with more zeros than a binary code live reading.

Miners, now, they're a unique breed. Like a group of ultra-dedicated sports enthusiasts who never miss a game, they're ensuring the ongoing health and speed of the Kaspa network. Harnessing the power of BlockDAG, the "blockchain but way better" evolution, they are expanding transaction processing, network security, and consensus mechanisms. They mine for the thrill of the hunt, and their honest work deters the baddest of actors.

Kaspa also has its eyes firmly set on the horizon, where the DAG KNIGHT protocol awaits like a shiny new software update. However, before it starts rejoicing with a metaphorical touchdown celebration and ushering in the era of smart contracts and Layer 2 solutions, there's another fascinating development in the works. Kaspa is currently sweating it out in the cyber gym, getting swole with its new Rust codebase.

The Rust rewrite isn't just another feather in Kaspa's cap; it's like a turbo-charger for the network speed. We're not talking about those measly 'Go faster' stripes you put on your car. It's swapping out the Go codebase for one coded with rocket fuel. The efficiency gains are not just impressive; they're through the roof.

Once Kaspa finalizes the Rust codebase, it'll be like unlocking a secret level in a video game. The doors to developing smart contracts and Layer 2 solutions will reveal a hidden path on World 2, presenting a warp whistle to fast travel into a greater DeFi ecosystem. There is still a long way until the final boss, but remember, all this is on the roadmap and destined to happen as if prophecy.

All this is happening with the GRO, or GrassRoots Organic community efforts and marketing, giving Kaspa a steady beat of drum rolls in the background. This isn't your typical communal and marketing efforts. It's more like an infectious tune you can't help but hum along to, spreading from one Kaspa user to another. Infecting the world with a pandemic of promise and greatness, an ensemble of crypto enthusiasts, developers, and users marching to the same beat. When challenges roll in, the community expands, welcoming fresh perspectives, ideas, and participants. As the tides recede, it contracts, streamlining its focus on specific tasks. This constant evolution mirrors the adaptive nature of the BlockDAG itself.

What Kaspa Does for Humanity

Everyone has a voice. Much like a grand assembly of network participants, the consensus protocol ensures that the more you contribute, the louder your voice echoes. This shared respect for hard work fuels the delicate dance of growth and adaptation, creating a living, breathing entity that never ceases to evolve. Kaspa is an audacious goal, an innovative technology, and a committed community, all coming together to write a new rulebook for finance.

When we talk about Kaspa, it's not just about the tech and the nifty buzzwords. It's about a mission that sounds like it was pulled from a high-stakes action movie: replacing traditional finance. Whether it's the high-rolling institutions or your friendly local store, Kaspa aims to take every part of it digital. It's like switching out your snail mail for email. All the value with none of the middlemen.

Kaspa, in the world of technology, is like that new, unfamiliar kitchen appliance you randomly receive as a gift. You know, the one that comes in the "As Seen on TV" tabloid-esque packaging with "cutting-edge technology" written all over it. At first, you're skeptical. What even is an air fryer?

But, once you pry open that box, not entirely sure what to expect, you are hit with a wave of excitement. This new gadget isn't merely an iteration of something familiar; it's an entire rethinking, a reimagining. You can make anything in this, from air-frying chicken nugs to grilled cheese to hard-air-fried eggs. You have been living your whole life wrong until now and are just finding out.

It's not just about creating a new technology; it's about what this technology can do for us. It's designed for adoption and inclusion, from the financial institutions on Wall Street to the guy at your local grocery store. Kaspa doesn't just want to be an alternative to traditional finance. No, that's too easy. Kaspa's audacious goal is not merely to be part of the world of finance but to transform it entirely. Its unrivaled network speed, coupled with the promise of Layer 2 solutions and smart contracts, positions it as an alternative to traditional finance and a successor. A tool built not just for the technologists but for the ordinary person. This tool brings financial transactions into the digital age.

In a world increasingly becoming decentralized, Kaspa stands unique. It doesn't just emulate the patterns of the old world within a new medium, it charts a new path, daring to reimagine the very bedrock of financial transactions and consensus. This daring approach, buoyed by a committed community, innovative technology, and an unwavering dedication to a shared vision sets Kaspa apart.

As Kaspa steps onto the PoW landscape, it's not just planting a flag; it's setting a new standard. It's demonstrating that it's possible to dream big and realize those dreams. It shows that the PoW trilemma is not a roadblock but an opportunity for innovation with the right approach.

Kaspa's achievement doesn't just redefine PoW; it takes a highlighter to the limitations and writes 'challenge accepted' in bold, uppercase letters. It's not about playing by the rules anymore; it's about writing a new rulebook altogether. Kaspa's move is a resounding checkmate in the grand chessboard of cryptocurrencies.

One thing I find fascinating about Kaspa is the peculiar overlap between the tech and the community. It's as if both the code and the people share the same DNA, making for an interesting symbiotic relationship. Like some kind of hybrid cyborg colony hellbent on upending traditional finance.

For instance, the blockDAG, Kaspa's backbone, is a vibrant, adaptable (almost living) entity, not just a linear chain. It morphs and adapts according to the demands of its environment. When transaction volumes surge, it sprawls out, expanding like a web to accommodate the influx, then contracts back to its original form when the storm subsides. Its movements are akin to a willow tree, expertly improvising and flowing with the cadence of the network's winds.

Mirroring the BlockDAG's dynamic adaptability is the Kaspa community, a constellation of crypto enthusiasts, developers, and users. Like the BlockDAG, it also adjusts its actions, size, and composition according to the governance needs. When faced with challenges, it expands and grows fervently, welcoming new solutions and perspectives. When the environment stabilizes, it contracts, concentrating on specific objectives. This organic entity is constantly evolving, adapting, and growing to meet the changing needs of the Kaspa ecosystem, forming an organic consensus protocol.

This dynamic relationship is guided by the Nakamoto ethos, a democratic system where every vote counts. Yet, unlike traditional democracies, it's not just about the number of people but the value of their contributions. The more effort a participant puts in, the greater their influence in the community's direction. This ethos resonates with Kaspa's PoW model, where the value of each contribution, each block of data, is measured by the work put into it. In both the Kaspa network and its community, the worth of one's voice is gauged by their effort and dedication. Kaspa runs on a proof-of-work protocol and community.

In the intricate ballet between Kaspa's tech and its community, both organisms reflect each other, growing and adapting in response to the other. This symbiotic relationship creates a virtuous cycle that keeps the Kaspa ecosystem healthy, robust, and constantly evolving. It bears evidence to the fact that when an effort is recognized and rewarded, the entire system thrives. This mutual respect for hard work and the resulting shared growth is the unique beauty of Kaspa and its community. This isn't just a tech platform and its user base--it's an ecosystem where technology and society mirror each other, each making the other stronger.

Now imagine walking into a room, except this room isn't just four walls and a ceiling. This room is a whole new reality, one where the rules are waiting to be bent, broken, and reshaped. That is Testnet 11. It's a brave new world for crypto exploration. If Kaspa is the captain of this ship, Testnet 11 is the uncharted waters it's venturing into.

Testnet 11 is just that; the 11th testnet. Launched on June 26, 2023, it's a public experimental network, and in layman's terms, it's an open playground for developers, crypto enthusiasts, and innovative minds. A place where they can put their heads together and stress-test various simulations, approaches, and ideas. It's a sandbox, but instead of sandcastles and cat feces, it's a construction site for the future of cryptocurrency.

This isn't your typical "*Wizard of Oz*, back scenes, smoke and mirror" kind of scenario. Kaspa, with Testnet 11, has invited every developer, user, and enthusiast to join the party. It's like a potluck where everyone brings their dish, only in this case, the dishes are CLI commands and computer resources.

So, what happens when you throw a bunch of passionate people into this groundbreaking testnet? Magic, that's what. And not just any magic, we're talking David Blaine levitation kind of magic, only without the illusions and fake tricks and the, well, levitation.

In the hands of this vibrant, innovative community, Testnet 11 became a crucible for Kaspa's success. These passionate members weren't just spectators in the crowd; they were players on the field. Every little experiment, nudge, and tweak helped shape the course of Testnet 11, steering it toward the groundbreaking achievement we're about to reveal.

They poured their efforts into Testnet 11, driving it, refining it, until it morphed into something more than a testnet. It became a steppingstone toward a landmark that would redefine the boundaries of cryptocurrency as we know it.

Ultimately, Testnet 11 is more than just a number and a word. It confirms the power of collective effort and the enchantment that happens when people come together for a shared goal. It embodies the saying that "the whole is greater than the sum of its parts."

If I asked you to think about scaling, you might picture yourself frantically clambering up a mountain. However, when it comes to cryptocurrency, scaling isn't about altitude or crampons. It's about expanding the potential, stretching the boundaries, and in Kaspa's case, making the seemingly impossible possible.

The landscape of cryptocurrency, until recently, was like trying to get a great white shark to walk on land. It had power and potential, but the limbs and lungs? Not so much. It was a world where security, decentralization, and scalability constantly jostled for space. And just when you thought you had a handle on one, the other two would throw a tantrum. It was a balancing act more precarious than a drunk uncle Eyal on a skateboard.

But then, along came Kaspa, ready to flip the script. Or rather, rewrite the entire play. With Testnet 11, Kaspa took the cryptocurrency landscape, shook it upside down, and chucked it into the 4th dimension.

Shai Deshe, our resident Kaspa quantum & cryptography researcher, shared a profound insight: "This is the first time a permissionless, public, proof-of-work network has demonstrated four-digit transaction rates directly on the consensus layer while running on affordable hardware. Some of the participants reported running on nine-year-old laptops! We are on track to prove that proof-of-work can actually scale just as well as proof-of-stake, but without the sacrifices to centralization and security. 3000 TPS was unexpectedly easy, pushing the limits, we might find that we can even outperform VISA."

Four-digit transactions! Outperform VISA! Nine-year-old laptops! I mean, most nine-year-old laptops can barely run a PowerPoint presentation without catching fire. But here they are, supporting a groundbreaking technological achievement, crushing world records, and giving VISA a run for its money. And you can participate, On. A. Laptop. That is unheard of transactional power, and still accessible and inclusive.

What Kaspa has achieved is no less than a revolution. It's shown us that PoW can actually scale just as well as PoS but without the sacrifices to centralization and security. It's a bit like finding out your pet turtle could do backflips this whole time. It shatters expectations and challenges what we thought we knew.

Shai's words give us a tantalizing glimpse into a future where cryptocurrencies are viable, efficient, powerful, and ready to rumble.

Yonatan Sompolinsky, Kaspa Founder and co-author of the GHOSTDAG protocol, who might as well wear a cape with the letter 'K' on it, maybe even a 'B,' too, when reflecting on the achievement, he said, "A 10 blocks/sec system is highly sensitive to minor errors or even suboptimal engineering; it requires a deep understanding of p2p consensus modules interplay and top-notch execution capabilities. I hope more devs will join the project, if anything, merely to enjoy the beauty manufactured."

So, here's a system that's more sensitive than a candle in a room full of floor fans. Now, add the enormous pressure of making it across the room, in the dark, with mousetraps strewn about, lying in wait to snatch onto your bare toes as soon as your only source of light goes out. Oh, and the room is full of naysayers, hecklers, and those weirdos who work at mall kiosks, always trying to sell you something you're not interested in. It's not for the weak-willed.

The technical ramifications of this endeavor are astounding. It isn't just about finding a quicker route to work; it's more akin to creating a wormhole that whisks you there in a heartbeat. It's comparable to a magic act where, in a startling twist, the rabbit miraculously pulls you out of the hat. And now, Sompolinsky opens the stage for other magicians-developers who seek the thrill of solving complex problems and the chance to be a part of a beautifully harmonized technological performance.

Michael Sutton, a distributed systems researcher & Kaspa core developer, reflected on the achievement, saying, "With the advent of GHOSTDAG as a scalable consensus protocol, we have reached a pivotal point where performance becomes paramount. Scaling a cryptocurrency is no longer constrained by the protocol; it now hinges on computation limits. Moreover, the powerful combination of widespread multi-core computers and the inherent parallelism opportunities of DAGs has allowed us to push the boundaries to their limits. This convergence of consensus and high-performance computing unlocks untapped potential, propelling us towards new horizons of research and innovation."

When you look at it like this, you start to see just what a monumental achievement this really is. This isn't just a giant unfathomable leap for Kaspa; it's supposed to be outright impossible. It's the day the rules got redefined, the block-barrier broken, and the bar got raised so high it's in geostationary orbit.

At this point, if you're not feeling at least a tiny bit exhilarated, I'd recommend checking your pulse. Because we're not just talking about a triumph here; we're talking about a game-changer. A tectonic shift in the cryptocurrency landscape that'll echo down the ages. A potential for a brand-new research field could stem from this accomplishment, and there is nothing to hold Kaspa back besides hardware. A limitation that constantly advances and becomes less of a restriction with each evolution.

We are now, definitively, venturing into uncharted territory. It's like finding a whole new wing in your house or discovering that hidden split-screen feature on your smartphone you never knew existed. It's the kind of thing that could lead to, well, the potentials are endless. But that's the beauty of it.

Breaking Records and Redefining What is Possible
In the wake of Kaspa's momentous achievement, the entire cryptocurrency market is abuzz. Not just abuzz. It's like a swarm of particularly excitable bees discovering a fresh bed of roses. After all, with 10 BPS, Kaspa has not just raised the bar; it's lifted it, thrown it up into the stratosphere, and waved it goodbye.

This achievement doesn't exist in a vacuum. It's as though Kaspa kicked open a door, and behind it lies a whole new realm of possibilities for other cryptocurrencies. Now, every Chad, Chris, and Satoshi is looking at Kaspa's achievement and thinking, "How..." It's the digital equivalent of the four-minute mile. Once thought impossible, now, it's the new benchmark.

As for future implications, well, your crystal ball is as good as mine. But let's take the liberty of a little educated speculation. We could be standing at the precipice of a new era of innovation and broader adoption.

When you make transactions as swift and easy as a tap dance and as secure as a Swiss vault, you're effectively removing barriers. Barriers that, till now, have held back many from embracing cryptocurrencies. But with Kaspa cracking the code, they've handed out a universal VIP pass.

In a world where speed, efficiency, and security are desirable and essential, a 10 BPS system isn't just an advancement; it's a revolution. And revolutions have a habit of spreading. So, don't be surprised if we soon see a wave of innovation and adoption that follows Kaspa's lead, like a fleet of ducklings trailing their mother.

The applications are vast, from governments looking to streamline their digital transactions to businesses wishing to optimize their systems and the general populace looking to see where their tax dollars go. And with every step toward optimization, the concept of digital currencies grows less and less alien. It's like the internet of the 90s--a fringe idea, then a fascinating novelty, and now, taken for granted and as essential as oxygen.

And one thing is for sure: Kaspa isn't done. The digital currency landscape is dynamic and ever-changing. Kaspa is built to adapt, evolve, and continue to leave us all awe-struck. Like a nimble-footed mountain goat navigating treacherous slopes, Kaspa is poised to maneuver whatever comes its way.

So, we've pulled back the curtain and unveiled the technological tour de force that is Kaspa. Ten Blocks Per Second is a tremendous achievement that if we gave it a physical form, it would probably need its own zip code or two.

The End of the Beginning

Kaspa is not merely about pushing technological boundaries; it's the realization of Satoshi Nakamoto's dream. A dream not confined by the limitations of current reality but a journey towards a future where the digital and the physical merge seamlessly, powered by a protocol that's solved blockchain trilemma without a single 404 error. This isn't your average 'reimagine and regurgitate' Bitcoin clone; this is a first-class ticket on the express train to a whole new digital age.

But remember, in the world of Kaspa, every ending is just a cleverly disguised beginning. As we close this book, somewhere in the digital entanglement of Kaspa's blockDAG, a new chapter is being written. So, while we revel in the magnitude of this 10 BPS triumph, rest assured, the Kaspa story is far from over. In fact, I'd venture to say it's just getting warmed up, with a promise of a future as electrifying as an ASIC, as promising as the Internet, and as fast as you can spend.

Coming up with chapter titles is way more complicated than it looks. Really, what this final chapter should have been titled is: "You're Here Early, and You're in for a Wild Ride."

Afterword

You made it! Well done. I suppose if you've gotten this far into the book, I can only assume that you are a sentient human being and not my cat walking across the keyboard, "accidentally" leaving me one-star reviews on Goodreads. If you are, in fact, my cat, kindly ignore the preceding statement, and please, for the love of Satoshi, let me sleep tonight.

You've been a loyal companion on this exhilarating journey into the heart of blockDAG, cryptographic hashes, and the multifaceted world of Kaspa. And you might wonder, "Is this the point where the author wraps up everything, extending gratitude for our perseverance, tying up loose ends, and sending us off with fond farewells?" To this, I respond, "Not yet, dear blockDAG aficionado. Not yet."

The Kaspa sphere operates like the ceaseless churning of a relentless tide. It's forever advancing, forever changing. Just when you think you've got a handle on it and reached a comfortable rhythm treading water, Kaspa ignites its turbocharged speedboat, leaving behind a dazzling wake of innovation. It's less about keeping stride now; it's more about marveling at the exhilarating speed and ingenuity of its evolution.

And now, let's take a dip into the Kaspa Ambassador Program. Imagine it as the United Nations of the Kaspa if the UN was a buzzing hive of crypto enthusiasts and not a sprawling bureaucratic machine. This program boldly brandishes a capital "D" for Decentralization on its metaphorical flag. It's a spontaneously organized GRO movement composed of individuals who've been bitten by the Kaspa bug and are hellbent on spreading it far and wide, irrespective of any potential WHO warnings. They've drunk the mana of the GHOSTDAG and want the world to taste it, too. A group that is diverse as they are dedicated, each bringing a unique perspective to the table, these ambassadors are essential gear in the intricate workings of the Kaspa ecosystem. They strive to expand and enrich their region's understanding of Kaspa, its capabilities, and its boundless potential in digital finance. Their infectious enthusiasm and tireless efforts are the spirit of decentralization and a foundational pillar of the Kaspa ethos.

At the helm of this endeavor is our very own 'Rhubarbarian.' Now, I don't know if he has an affinity for tart pies or if he's a descendant of the infamous Canadian Barbarian tribes of old. What I do know, however, is that he's the one who got this party started. He knew that if Kaspa were to be the people's crypto, it had to be spread by the people, for the people. So, he lit the spark, stoked the fire, and soon, the Ambassador Program was born.

And boy, has the wildfire grown. Each ambassador is not just a representative but a fervent evangelist armed with an unwavering dedication to manifest Kaspa's groundbreaking potential. They are the torchbearers, the pathfinders, illuminating the way to a future that once seemed confined to the fanciful realms of speculative fiction.

For example, let's zero in on Uganda, where we find a gentleman named Mugisha. I haven't met the man yet, but I can tell already he's what I'd call a

'Kaspa Renaissance man.' No need for an inflated collar or feathered cap. Mugisha juggles roles as an Ethereum scholar, community outreach maestro, and crypto advisor. And as of May 2023, he's donned a new hat as Kaspa's Ambassador in Uganda.

But don't let the formal title deceive you. Mugisha's daily itinerary isn't filled with luncheons or ceremonial ribbon cuttings. He's a dynamo, his day-to-day more resembling a time-lapse video than a quiet pastoral scene. He's ceaselessly nurturing the growth of the Kaspa community in Uganda, stoking the embers of curiosity and fuelling the flames of technological enlightenment.

His every action is a ripple in the Kaspa pond, each one setting off a chain reaction that further propels Kaspa's vision in Uganda. But Mugisha is more than just riding this wave of innovation and community-building. He's out there with a shovel and a pail, constructing the very sands upon which these waves break. He's a builder, an architect of a monument that manifests technological progress in a way that's as tangible as the book in your hand.

Imagine this scenario: Your neighbor, whom you've always admired from a distance (nothing creepy, just wholesome admiration for their lush, weed-free lawn), invites you over for a barbeque. And not just any barbeque, but a feast of epic proportions. You can already smell the savory smoke, feel the warmth of the welcoming smile, and taste the tang of the secret recipe BBQ sauce. But there's one problem - there's a gorge separating the two properties. Don't worry; your neighbor has thought of this and built a sturdy, architecturally sound bridge just for you.

That, in a nutshell, is the Kaspa to Ethereum bridge. Only replace the barbeque with the alluring array of DeFi services on Ethereum, and swap the gorge with the chasm of technological incompatibility. The bridge is live, and it's a game-changer.

And the construction workers behind this digital Bifröst are everyday ecosystem developers looking to integrate Kaspa further into their platform! They dusted off their virtual hard hats, grabbed their digital pickaxes and shovels, and got down to business. The result? A user-friendly, thoroughly-engineered bridge that lets you take Kaspa and wrap it up in a neat little package to carry across to Ethereum. We're talking about Wrapped Kaspa, or wKAS, if you're into the whole brevity thing.

This bridge, or digital portal, is like a 24/7 passport office, granting visa-free access to the DeFi Disneyland that is Ethereum. It opens the gates to a realm of lending, borrowing, yield farming, and all the nifty crypto jibber jabber I've been rambling on about in this book. But it's not a one-way road. Ethereum explorers can also skip across to the Kaspa side to dip their toes in its refreshing waters.

Just when you thought you'd swallowed the last mouthful of Kaspa's groundbreaking progression, it serves up another generous helping. And just when you think you've got a handle on things, Kaspa leaps forward in innovation - more of a boxing kangaroo than a predictable gym rat on a treadmill. This techno-marathon, however, isn't running out of steam; it's ramping up the pace. It's time to gear up for another landmark event – the subsequent launch of a spanking new Rust testnet. It still has that fresh Rust smell and will soon be complete with its own visualizer.

So you're no longer a passive passenger; you've been promoted to the pilot's seat. You have a panoramic view of the intricate network of Kaspa transactions, a view hitherto reserved for the tech wizards behind the curtain. You're now privy to the vibrant masterpiece of the blockDAG, with nodes blooming like digital daisies and transactions zipping by at breakneck speeds. It's like being thrust into the heart of a synchronized swimming performance, except here, it's not swimmers but code. Yet, both still don't know what they're doing or why they're doing it.

It's going to be every bit as enthralling as watching a high-speed, high-stakes game of Frogger where the score doesn't matter. Because in the grand scheme of things, we're all winners here. Each node, each transaction, and each line of code is proof of innovation, the sheer audacity of the Kaspa project, and you, yeah, you, get to be a part of it. Isn't that something?

The beauty of this journey is that we're still exploring. We're still navigating the expanse of what digital finance, and particularly Kaspa, can offer us. The story continues to unfold, with each page-turning faster than the one before. If you don't keep up, you might wake up tomorrow and find Kaspa has already built a utopian haven on the moon. Okay, probably not the moon, but you get the drift.

After delving into the riveting world of Kaspa, serving as the scribe of its grand narrative, and perhaps even becoming a little/lot obsessed, I decided to take things a step further. You know, to channel my seemingly inexhaustible enthusiasm for all things Kaspa into an endeavor that felt more personal, more explorative.

Thus, Parameterless.io was born. A newsletter, nay, a digital canvas where I can let my voice echo more freely, unrestrained by the formal protocols of Kaspa Currency Medium articles. Think of it as the diary of a Kaspa enthusiast, replete with my musings, experiences, and stories from this exhilarating journey.

What can you expect from Parameterless.io? Well, to start, quirky tales about Kaspa. Because let's face it, the crypto world can be as fascinating as it is mind-boggling. It's an expedition of tech jargon, blockDAG nuances, and digital controversies. And somewhere in the mix, there are real people with real stories worth telling.

I aim to shine a spotlight on these stories. To peel back the layers of technobabble and reveal the human side of Kaspa. You'll meet the faces behind the names and hear about the triumphs, the setbacks, and everything in between. You'll be at the front of the narrative unfolding in real-time, from the rise of new Kaspa merchants to the roll-out of ecosystem features that even Cyberpunk would be impressed by.

So, welcome to Parameterless.io. It's a peek into my brain, a fireside chat in the vast, digital wilderness of Kaspa. A place to gather, learn, and share in the excitement of this new frontier. Also serving as a testbed for an alternative method of raising KAS for the Community Marketing Fund, currently incentivizing just my fellow writers.

Now, you're probably mulling over all this Kaspa-mania, perhaps even contemplating how you can hitch a ride on this digital rocket. Well, here's some friendly advice from one Kaspa enthusiast to another. Dive in. Start by getting your feet wet; the Discord is a perfect first stop. Engage with the community, ask questions, and learn. It might seem daunting, but remember, we were all novices once. You don't need a Ph.D. in Cryptography or Computer Science to be part of the Kaspa community. What you need is curiosity, an open mind, and a readiness to step out of your comfort zone and be willing to accept Kaspa is an entirely different class of crypto. And finally, stay vigilant. Keep up-to-date with the latest developments and accomplishments. Kaspa isn't a static project; it's a living, breathing entity that is constantly evolving. To be part of Kaspa is to be part of an ongoing expedition.

Here we are, well into the information age, where your toaster is smart enough to join a Zoom meeting, and your refrigerator is capable of giving you dietary advice; Kaspa reminds us that we're barely scratching the surface of what technology can do. In this story, we're all explorers, trailblazing a new crypto landscape, trying to keep up with Kaspa's high-speed rocketship that seemingly knows no end.

You've got to admire Kaspa's spirit. It reminds me of that kid in school who'd always raise their hand, bursting with questions, no matter how late the hour was. But instead of being irksome and holding up the class with a last-minute question, Kaspa's hand goes up with solutions, advancements, and new pathways. The constant flow of innovation, community building, and global integration makes one thing clear - Kaspa isn't just changing the game; it's building a new one altogether.

Before we conclude this tale, a heartfelt tip of the hat to a diverse and dynamic group who made this journey both exhilarating and enlightening. To the spirited Kaspa community – enthusiasts, developers, contributors, and visionaries – your collective energy and commitment have been a constant source of inspiration. You've made this an enjoyable adventure, one that continues to defy expectations. Special recognition is due to those individuals who kickstarted this incredible venture and continue to fuel its momentum. Their dedication is the engine propelling Kaspa forward, paving the way for a brighter and more inclusive digital future.

Equally significant are the countless silent members of the Kaspa community, often without a voice but never unappreciated, who don their virtual hard hats daily. Some trade, some hodl, some transact, while others prefer to lurk and observe from the sidelines. Together, they ensure Kaspa's network continues functioning as designed, thus making its intended use case a reality. These quiet participants, through their everyday use and belief in the system, are proof of the robustness and reliability of Kaspa. Each one of you, in various capacities and from different corners of the globe, has been integral to this journey. Your engagement, be it active or passive, forms the foundation upon which Kaspa stands today. Your spirit is the essence of Kaspa. This book is not just a tribute to a transformative project; it is an homage to all of you, everyday users.

Let's not forget that the narrative of Kaspa is far from over. The future glimmers with the same thrilling anticipation one might associate with a solar-powered ice cream maker. This isn't just a fanciful metaphor; it's a reality unfolding in real-time, promising exciting and transformative change. Whether you're a tech enthusiast, a crypto trader, or even a discerning reader, stay engaged and vigilant. With Kaspa, the journey ahead is shaping up to be a riveting expedition, one that invites us to look forward with hope and enthusiasm.

So, I'm signing off here. As I bow out of this saga, I just want to say that I believe that everything Kaspa is and stands for is precisely what Satoshi Nakamoto envisioned for Bitcoin. Maybe there's even more to this...

Thanks for reading!

239 N. R. Crowningshield

Kaspa Contributors

Thanks to all who made Kaspa and this book a reality.

The Founder
Yonatan Sompolinsky (hashdag)

Core Developers & Researchers
Elichai Turkel (elichai2)
Michael Sutton (msutton)
Mike Zak (svarog)
Ori Newman (someone235)
Shai Wyborski (deshe)

Marketing, Business Dev. & Listings
Avidan Abitbol (Avidan)
Chad Ballantyne (Rhubarbarian)
Chris Wolf (Wolfie)

Community Contributors

Adam (CoinProspector)
Allan_QuartermainSr
allii
Amao (Amao)
Anton Yemelyanov (aspect)
Azazino
azbuky
AvogHadro
Bape
Ben
B, Smith (Miner_League)
Cafalchio (CafaBr)
Chris Hopium
CHRIS45 | NEW
Coderofstuff
colinfran
CressonMiningCo
Cøcønut Shark
CryptoK
Dablacksplash
Daniel
D-Stacks (JWJ on github)
Dmitry
DOUGLAS Hayse
Edward (cryptoarmy)
fishtuna
Frnf
Gavin Wood (GWood)
Georges Künzli (Tiram)
Guy Corem
hanpaopao
Helix
IceCreamFish
imalfect

James Wraith
Jason Dixon (titorelli)
KaffinPX
Kaspa Silver
Kingu
Lazzeruz
Mert (Mertery)
MoonShotJosh
Mr.solomon
Moomin is awesome
Navin Tiwary (icecreamfish)
Oisin
Oudeis
Panchuker (lab_cripto)
pbfarmer
pennywiize
Porventura
Potat
Raphael
Ratstang
Rilragos
Robert Matejko (IAmeR^)
sa1krishna
Splinter
SudoSi
supertypo
Surinder Singh Matoo (Matoo)
Taipei
The AllFather
Tim
Tmrlvi (hauntedcook)
TreeBrother
tug
Wolf9466

Links

Website: kaspa.org

Kaspa Wiki: wiki.kaspa.org

KGI (Visualizer): kgi.kaspad.net

GitHub: github.com/kaspanet

Twitter: twitter.com/KaspaCurrency

Medium: medium.com/kaspa-currency

Reddit: reddit.com/r/kaspa

Discord: discord.gg/kaspa

Telegram: t.me/Kaspaenglish

The Kaspa Developer Fund

kaspa:precqv0krj3r6uyyfa36ga7s0u9jct0v4wg8ctsfde2gkrsgwgw8jgxfzfc98

The Community Marketing Fund

kaspa:qpyr8yp7jmantyaatyqtpwuzv3fcthe2r7jz6n55nl4hdd0288e8jljunnqgv

A Parameterless Story

The Saga of Potat

The Potato That Defied All Odds. In the digital town hall of the Kaspa Telegram, a series of events rolled out that would add a new chapter to my understanding of the virtual world and its peculiarities. The catalyst was an unexpected private message, a tiny drop in the vast ocean of digital communication, yet containing the seed that would sprout into an unforgettable journey. The messenger was none other than Potat, an online entity I'd recognized through chatter in the Kaspa Telegram group and, unbeknownst to me at the time, Discord. However, we hadn't really had a direct dialog until that moment.

Potat, a figure who always stood out as a virtuoso in the Kaspa technical arena, boasted an understanding of blockDAG and the protocol that made my knowledge look like a kiddie pool next to the Pacific. I had launched the Kaspa Currency Medium not long before, and it was just taking off. Potat, being the ever-watchful Kaspa enthusiast he was, must've picked up on this. So, when he pinged me with a proposition as audacious as trying to reverse-engineer a TOOL song from Lateralus, it was as surprising as it was thrilling.

Our goal was to probe the black hole known as Reddit, specifically the r/cryptocurrency forum, and spread the good word about Kaspa, our champion digital currency. At the time, Kaspa was fresh off the blocks on MEXC, and our community was beginning to germinate. This particular subreddit, known for its snobbish attitude and preference for heavyweight coins, was a tough sell. The whole venture was shot in the dark but fueled by digital courage and a sprinkle of insanity, YOLO.

And so, Potat and I found ourselves rallying together in this online crusade, thrown into the chaos by the unpredictable whirlpool of the Internet. The path ahead was less a road and more a goat track, and we stumbled and fumbled our way through. Despite language barriers, miscommunication, and my initial blunders in navigating the subreddit, we pushed ahead, our shared passion and zeal shaping our efforts to craft a post that would meet the often nitpicky standards of r/cryptocurrency.

The D-day finally arrived, the day our collective brainchild would face the scrutiny of the r/cryptocurrency subreddit. My heart rate remained relatively normal. I kept my expectations in check, aware that our creation was a tiny raft in a sea of clickbait, obnoxious voices, and trending hot topics. My newbie status on the subreddit held us back, preventing me from posting. The baton was now in Potat's hand—a plot twist we hadn't foreseen but one we had to adapt to.

Potat stepped up to the plate, bravely sharing our message on the roller-coaster ride that is Reddit's discussion platform. I was all set for our lovingly crafted argument to get lost in the avalanche of dog and Elon meme tokens and rug pulls. Yet, to my surprise, our post didn't just create a few ripples—it caused a tsunami. Upvotes piled up like a flash mob, each one endorsing our content, pushing it higher up the ranks. It was like watching a tiny snowball turn into an avalanche, gathering momentum at every turn. The rising figures—100, 200, 500, 1000—hit me like a brick to the face. Each update, excitedly pinged by Potat over

Telegram, slowly shifted my initial skepticism to a state of stunned disbelief. Our quiet collaboration had transformed into a virtual powerhouse—a demonstration of online platforms' untamed power and collective passion.

This unexpected success felt like discovering a hidden stash of fries at the bottom of a fast-food bag—pure, unadulterated joy. We transitioned from regular Internet dwellers to astronauts making first contact in an alien digital world. Kaspa community members caught wind, and probably half of our online members were now active in the subreddit. We were swept up in a whirlwind of engagement and curiosity, responding to intrigued Redditors, sifting through a deluge of comments, and participating in brain-stimulating debates.

However, the digital cosmos, like the market, has a way of reestablishing equilibrium, often with a cosmic explosion's swift and brutal force. Our triumph was abruptly halted when our magnum opus—our joint labor of love—was unceremoniously deleted. The doors of the r/cryptocurrency forum were slammed in our faces, and we were labeled as "brigadiers." The self-appointed guardians declared Kaspa, the subject of our discourse, a "shitcoin." We were cryptoblocked by self-proclaimed crypto enthusiasts.

As if things weren't already absurd enough, several stalwart users of r/cryptocurrency, including Potat, were slapped with permanent bans.

This was the worst part. Potat was a devoted user with years invested in the subreddit. It should have been my liability, but the karma nonsense wrote his fate in code. He didn't even get a last meal or a goodbye letter; he was just booted out with all the ceremony of throwing a trash bag in a dumpster.

The irony of being scolded for discussing a specific cryptocurrency on a forum explicitly designed for such discussions was as striking as absurd. It felt like test-flying a plane and realizing no landing gear was installed mid-flight. Yet, as the shock of our ejection quickly faded, when I realized something significant. The fervent pushback from the moderators was an indirect acknowledgment of Kaspa's potential, which was too substantial to be ignored. A coin this advanced and new, generating such buzz, can't be good for the health of already dying assets.

Our expulsion from r/cryptocurrency set the stage for an awkward return to the Discord and Telegram. As if an asteroid flung from a gravity assist, we were thrown into a universe of mixed responses and controversy. Upon returning to the familiar territory of the Kaspa subreddit, the community celebrated the event as a victory, as shocking as our virality had been. For a flash, Kaspa was thrust into the limelight for reasons as unpredictable as Chaos Theory, and just as unpredictably, we returned to welcoming excitement and shared stories of the adventure.

In the immediate aftermath of our banishment, an unexpected sequence of events unfolded, eerily resembling a scene pulled right out of the historical epic, '300'. Allan_QuartermainSr, a stout-hearted champion of our community, stepped forward, refusing to bow to the dictatorial tendencies of the r/cryptocurrency moderators. Embodying the same unyielding spirit as his mighty Spartans against the massive Persian army, he confronted the bloated allegations of "brigading" head-on. In a show of digital defiance that would make even Leonidas proud, he fiercely defended our Kaspa community, refusing to let the waves of undue criticism and misinformation dismantle our Reddit phalanx.

Just as the dust of this digital battlefield started to settle, Allan_QuartermainSr swiftly and suddenly changed his stance to that of ancient historian Herodotus and began to document our saga. He meticulously etched every skirmish, every accusation, and every retort into the annals of our shared digital history, treating each instance with the gravity of a significant historical event.

So wait - Stop here for a minute - Actually, picture this. A keyboard warrior version of King Leonidas fighting with the ferocity of a feral honeybadger. "This is Kaspa!" The battle ends; he throws down his spear and shields for pen and paper and starts chronicling with all the enthusiasm of an eager scholar. "Hmm, what a fascinating turn of events for the history books!"

The ensuing dispute reflected the broader conflict in the crypto world— the tension between centralization and decentralization, control and freedom. Our audacious venture into r/cryptocurrency, our untimely dismissal, and the unexpected fame and support that followed were enlightening. It initiated a conversation about the essence of cryptocurrency. It challenged the capricious power wielded by those who sought to control the narrative.

But at the end of the day, the whole escapade made me appreciate the power of our community, the influence of collective passion, and the untamed unpredictability of the digital landscape. Whether it was Potat's passion for technology or Allan_QuartermainSr's digital defiance, each of us played a role in creating a slice of Kaspa history. It revealed that when united, even a small team of crypto misfits from around the world could shake up the digital world. Even if just for a moment.

If you enjoyed this Parameterless story, you can check out more captivating tales about our vibrant community, thriving ecosystem, dedicated merchants, and all things Kaspa! To never miss a chapter, subscribe to the parameterless.io newsletter.

About the Author

N.R. Crowningshield: sleep-deprived new parent, keyboard warrior, and the equivalent of "that guy who always shows up at awkward times" in the Kaspa community. His headfirst plunge into Kaspa was triggered by the complex allure of the Kaspa Graph Inspector. It was a bewitching spectacle that felt like love at first sight or that tingle you get when you suspect black magic. Finding no comprehensive 'How to Kaspa for Dummies' guide, he created one himself, leading to the birth of the Kaspa Currency Medium page.

In this process, he took a literary leap of faith, transitioning from crafting science fiction to wrestling with the stubborn non-fiction facts of crypto. Like trying to swap from prose to code, he probably shouldn't, but he did it anyway. Now, if only he could figure out why Shai has yet to accept his friend request in Discord...

nrcrowningshield.com

www.ingramcontent.com/pod-product-compliance
Lightning Source LLC
Chambersburg PA
CBHW072141290526
45794CB00004B/1382